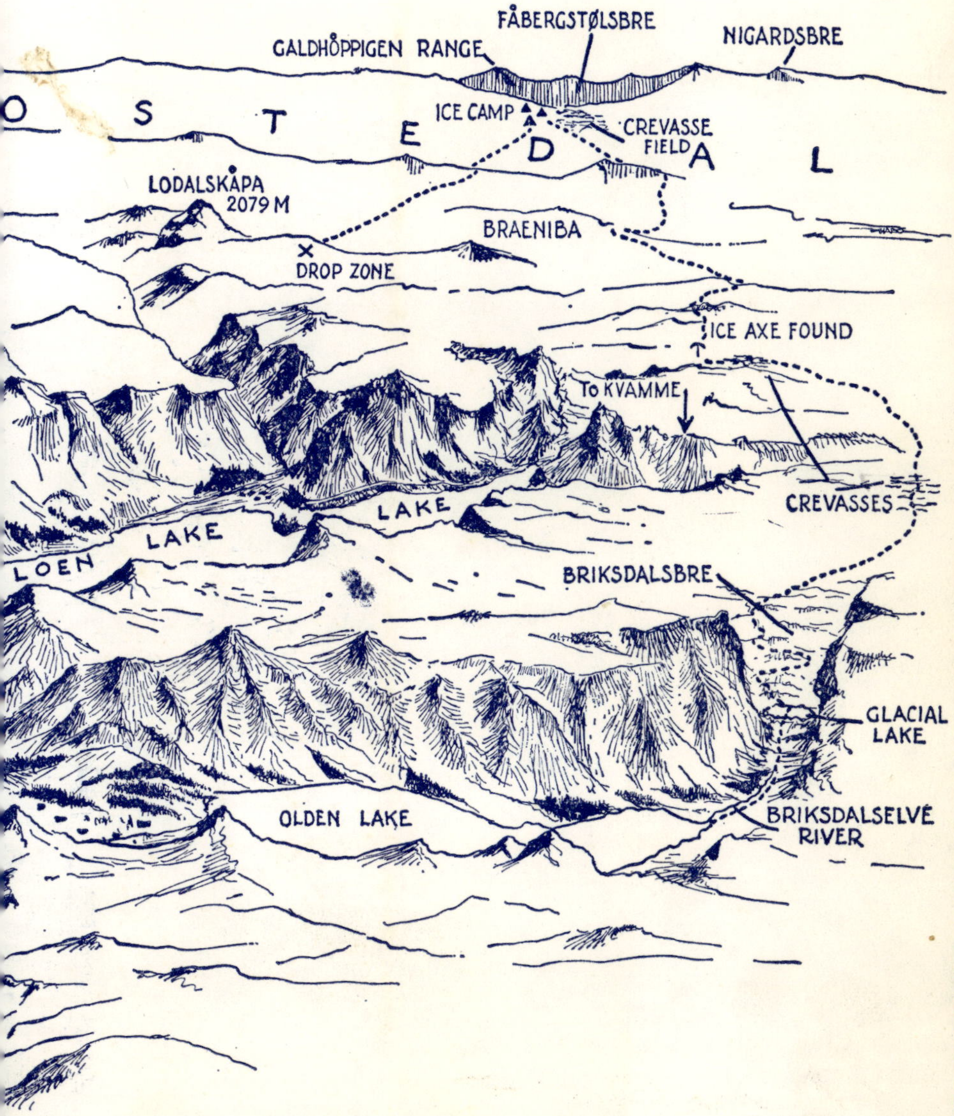

GALDHÖPPIGEN RANGE
FÅBERGSTØLSBRE
NIGARDSBRE
O S T E D A L
ICE CAMP
CREVASSE FIELD
LODALSKÅPA 2079 M
BRAENIBA
DROP ZONE
ICE AXE FOUND
To KVAMME
CREVASSES
LOEN LAKE
LAKE
BRIKSDALSBRE
GLACIAL LAKE
OLDEN LAKE
BRIKSDALSELVE RIVER

Ice Fall in Norway

Also by Ranulph Fiennes

A TALENT FOR TROUBLE

Sir Ranulph Twisleton-Wykeham-Fiennes

Ice Fall in Norway

HODDER AND STOUGHTON
LONDON SYDNEY AUCKLAND TORONTO

 First printed 1972. ISBN 0 340 15534 5.
 Printed in Great Britain for Hodder and Stoughton Limited, St. Paul's House, Warwick Lane, London, EC4P 4AH by Richard Clay (The Chaucer Press), Ltd., Bungay, Suffolk

For my Mother

for years of encouragement

Then we rounded the last bend and saw the Jostedal. It stood high up at the end of the fjord, very white in contrast to the green of the water and the still brighter green of the valley grass bathed in sunshine; it was a beautiful and terrifying sight.

HAMMOND INNES – *The Blue Ice*

Contents

Illustrations

Key to acknowledgments:

All photographs by the author, except

1 Erik Berglund, Birkhaug & Omdal Bergens Tidende.

2 Brendan O'Brien

Maps

ONE

N.G.2.

In the deep forest, twigs cracked beneath the scrabbling claws of unseen birds, a family of wild boar lolloped with ungainly grace through the low sea of bog cotton, and the mellow patter of raindrops on a mossy carpet accentuated the heavy silence after the rain.

Pea-green mildew clung to a low sign on the edge of the forest rimmed by heath. The words were obscured but once had warned the passing poacher: PRIVAT. EINGANG STRENG VERBOTEN.

Now a kiebitz mewed plaintively, jinking low as it passed the sign, for it saw movement in the dark deciduous scrub below the pines. Perhaps a fox or marten stirred within the shadows of the tangled vegetation; but it was too early yet for the predators.

A lean grey squirrel high above the undergrowth stared downwards from its leafy crow's nest. It was not deceived. A high vibrating whine, as of many geese in flight, whirred overhead and the squirrel flinched, not understanding.

The khaki helicopter with its flashing bubble of cockpit glass banked hard over the edge of the forest, an observer straining his eyes along the green flank, missing little. He saw the point of whiteness was only a signpost and nodded to the pilot. The machine veered away and was gone.

The squirrel relaxed but still its little orange eyes peered fixedly below.

Surely the thickness of the gloom contained movement as though men were treading warily. There was a clink of heavy metal and then a low voice speaking in a language which the German squirrel did not recognise.

'Och, that was neer, but I bet the bustard nivver caught the wee-est sight of us. Can we come up top, Mister Feens? It's awfu' cold doon here and it's a guid two hours since our last Naafi break. Scratch, why d'you no make some mair tatty sannies? I'm fair starving.'

A deeper voice sounded, equally disembodied.

'Why don't you shut yer mooth, Zeebo, there's nay mair breed, and there's nay mair tatties, so you can do us all a favour by piping doon and wrapping up.'

I was shivering with the damp and cursing the day I had joined the army. True, if one had to be in a tank regiment, there was none better than the Scots Greys. My Father had been killed in the last war whilst commanding them. Then there had been a war, a great cause to fight for and die for. But now, in the early sixties, only endless repetitive weeks of tedious manoeuvres in dank forests and over rolling plains – hopelessly eroded by the churning metal tracks of countless other mock tank battles.

It was late summer now and my little troop of three Centurions was but a part of a vast NATO advance on the Weser. The enemy, somewhere on the other bank, were the Danes and the French – as far as I could make out from the over-complicated blurb of instructions we had all been given the week before.

So far we had rolled south through the central rural belt of Prussia for some two hundred miles, tearing up tarmac roads, ripping through fences and ploughing through ripe wheat fields, without seeing any signs of the 'enemy'.

The one redeeming factor of these exercises was the solid quality of my tank crew: Scratch Sherville the ungainly operator, Zeebo Stevens the ever-hungry gunner, and Ian Durrand the driver – and the best mechanic who ever got lost under the engine decks of a Centurion. We were generally acknowledged to be the dirtiest crew in the regiment, but by private consensus we were also by far the most efficient.

The metallic tones of the squadron leader came from the headsets.

'Hello 24, this is 2. Ripe Fräulein Now. Over.'

Scratch scrabbled feverishly amongst a heap of half-empty food tins, 'nudey' magazines, and cigarette stubs, cursing as he grabbed for the headsets and microphone and passed them across the breech to me.

'Hello 2, this is 24. Ripe Fräulein Now. Out to you. Hello all stations 24. Acknowledge. Over.'

Somewhere farther along the edge of the same wood my sergeant and corporal in their respective tanks were doubtless prodded awake by their operators, and tersely acknowledged the code word for a general advance.

Durrand had heard the message, and there came a shattering roar as the Mark VI Centurion started up. Two pine trees, some sixty feet high, splintered like matchwood and crashed between our clattering tracks as Durrand deftly flicked through the gearbox and the tank lurched from the forest.

Bound by bound, in a leap-frogging movement, the three tanks moved forward, and, for many miles to either flank, other metal monsters – many carrying infantry – advanced through the fields of ripe corn towards the thin brown line of the Weser winding through the wide valley.

The village sign said MÜHLENDORF AM WESER. There was no sign of life. We must reach a concealed position on the very banks of the river, but carefully cropped hedges or garden fencing edged the road. Then there appeared a wide gravel drive with a gate standing open. We crunched left with a shrill whine of the steering brakes, as Durrand turned the 50-ton tank in neutral. The tarmac road was chewed up, and the gate-post disappeared.

Through a low apple orchard, and into a high hay-storage barn which blocked the way to the river. It should provide an excellent view of all immediate approaches to the other bank, for its far side was not walled. The interior was gloomy but there appeared to be no obstruction.

A sudden wild squealing rose above the engine noise and a crackling of split wood. But Durrand edged on into the barn coming to a halt only when the ugly snout of our 20-pounder pointed out of the barn with 180 degrees of unobstructed traverse.

Zeebo began to plant hay over our machine by way of concealment when I heard him exclaim with delight.

'D'you see what you've been and done, Durrand? Will you just take a luik behind your wagon. You've fair filled the larder for us for the rest of the exercise. We'll be eating like lairds fer the next week, so we will!'

As my eyes became accustomed to the poor light, I saw that Zeebo was holding the mangled remains of a small porker in his bloody hands and grinning delightedly.

A plump frau arrived to view the devastation. The barn had been used as a pen for a litter of piglets. Two of the eight were still alive and squealing.

'Verzeihung,' I apologised to the woman who was now weeping and wringing her podgy hands, 'sondern wir haben die Schweinen im Schatten gar nicht gesehen.'

Durrand, diplomatic as ever, arrived silently with cigarettes and ration tins. The frau sobbed fitfully and continued to mutter Teutonic oaths of vengeance on the 'verdamten Engländer'.

'Get it right, lass,' murmured Durrand, 'we're Scots, not Sassenachs, except for Mister Feens here.'

She took the goodies in her grubby apron and scurried off to find Fritz.

Secretly she must be hoping her whole barn would fall down, for the damage compensation claimed by the Germans was always monstrously above the actual cost of the repairs required – whether to gardens or wheat crops. The claims were always met, and we had little doubt that, in this case, the gateway of the drive had been purposefully left open – an invitation for our entry.

The battle continued, but we never saw the opposition. We were after all just pawns in a greater scheme of things and, as the months and the years passed, the exercises went on with little change.

I met friends in other regiments posted to such far-flung spots as Sarawak, Sharjah and Hong Kong. They were the lucky ones; savouring the fascination of the east whilst we floundered in the Prussian mire learning and seeing little new from year to year.

Bored with this monotonous existence and eager to travel, I

began to spend my annual leaves in Norway, usually with a friend and a canoe. By our fourth visit we had come to know the rivers and fjords of central Norway fairly well. The part of Norway which interested us most was the Jotunheim area which contains the largest snowfield in Europe. From this shimmering table-cloth of ice and snow many valley glaciers descend, the largest and most magnificent being the Jostedal, a massive vertical splendour of giant blocks of ice, tumbling haphazard down giddy cliffs to the lakes below. These gleaming slabs are for ever shifting; moaning and grinding, in tortured response to the intolerable stresses of gravity. From the lakes at the base of these frozen rivers issue raging torrents which race down the valleys to the calmer levels of the fjords and so to the sea.

In 1965 a friend and I planned to canoe from the western mountains to Oslo, starting our journey immediately below the Jostedal glacier. This river journey to Oslo proved to be a wild dash through magnificent country but we had completed less than a third of our intended route when our last remaining canoe was dashed to pieces in a cataract and lost.

Despite this failure, Norway still lured me back, for standing at the foot of the Jostedal glacier before canoeing off to Oslo, I had peered up at the great ice-cliffs soaring above and wondered what the plateau which caused such glacial outpourings might be like. I knew that there were routes up to the plateau if you were fit and knew where to look for them, and that trails existed that led right over the ice-fields from the side of the sea fjords to inland eastern Jotunheim. Once herds of cattle and the famous fjord ponies were driven over these 'drift' trails, for they had formed vital trade links between the coast and inland Norway. I learnt that the last 'drift' of animals was taken across the ice in 1857, but that then the gently sloping edges of the tongues leading up to the plateau began to melt and recede and their slopes became too steep and dangerous for the animals.

So, in 1967, six of us decided to explore the Jotunheim by following one of the old trails right across the plateau and then to canoe down the river running from the Jostedal *bre* or glacier. Only this time we would take with us canoes of different designs and varying materials to test out which was the sturdiest for these raging icy torrents which curved through the rock.

By chance all those participating in this journey in 1967 were parachutists. We estimated that we could save at least four days from our precious army leave and the considerable effort of climbing up on to the ice plateau if we parachuted on to the Jostedalsbre. The plan would be to charter a Norwegian plane from Bergen and drop with all our equipment including skis, then we would attempt to locate a drift trail, without a guide, and follow it off the glacier to the east where there is a little hamlet named Ǒysaeter. The *saeter* huts are situated where our chosen river begins its descent to the fjords and the sea.

We made the journey in August 1967. The parachute drop went as planned and was a great success; mainly owing to the leadership and expertise of Don Hughes, the chief instructor of the Netheravon Parachute School in England. The Jostedalsbre is notorious for its bad weather and for the deep crevasses which cut across it; but that August the weather was clear and calm when we jumped and the previous winter had been severe, so thick snow covered the crevasses and made a soft landing possible. No one was injured.

However, we failed to follow the complete course of a drift trail, partly because the equipment was too heavy and partly, since three of the team were weak skiers, because the combination of thick snow, high altitude and heavy packs proved too much. Nor did the canoeing fare much better than the ski-ing, for all the canoes proved unsatisfactory and foundered in the rapids before reaching the lower fjords.

Nevertheless the expedition had not proved a complete failure and the experience taught us a great deal. We realised that if we were to make such a journey again everyone taking part must be trained in parachuting, langlauf or cross-country ski-ing and canoeing, and that the equipment would have to be 'sledged' not carried on our backs. Moreover, we thought that specially modified rubber boats with extra protective linings would prove the most likely craft to navigate the hard jagged rocks, for they might bounce off or over obstacles rather than crashing into them. Better equipment next time would mean a more expensive venture; financing it might prove quite a problem.

We finished the expedition full of ideas but with little likelihood of our being able to get together again to carry them out for quite a while. I was still determined to cross the Jostedalsbre one day and to descend one of the magnificent glaciers and its river to the sea; but for the present it would have to wait.

Soon afterwards I left for the Middle East to join the Sultan of Muscat's Army. After a year I was due six weeks leave, which, for a number of reasons, I spent in North Africa ascending the course of the White Nile in two mini-hovercraft. Owing to delays imposed by sandstorms and an early rain season, as well as political trouble due to the Arab–Israeli war, I arrived back for duty in Dhofar some two months late. However, the Colonel was of a generous disposition and understood that leave from such out of the way armies as the Sultan's, can be, by the will of Allah, of a nebulous and elastic duration.

Back from the Nile regions, with only a year of army life ahead, the reality of 'civvi street' loomed large during the long desert nights. The cool sand was a soft bed, and the clear spangled sky was blotting paper to a thousand wild hopes and dreams of possible careers, just one of which might some day find fruition.

One scheme which I felt might be worth a try was prompted by a side effect of the Nile journey. Although various firms like British Petroleum and Horlicks had helped us considerably, the expedition had incurred a large financial loss. On the other hand, the firm which had loaned us the two mini-hovercraft had, as a result of the Nile journey, gained over ten million pounds sterling in export orders. On our way up the Nile we had staged hover demonstrations at major towns such as Khartoum – where the President and a crowd of five thousand had watched the craft – Malakal, and Kampala on Lake Victoria.

It seemed reasonable to think that this exporting success could be repeated with other British firms. If I were to organise expeditions using loaned materials and in turn test and advertise the equipment on behalf of the sponsors, the arrangement should be mutually beneficial.

Such expeditions would be trade missions with a difference, and if all the equipment required could be obtained in this manner there need be no repetition of the financial disaster of the Nile journey. The basic theme would be research both into equipment and into natural phenomena, and we would go wherever further scientific knowledge of the environment was needed –

B

from the sand ergs of the Sahara to the brash-ice of the Kara Sea.

Britain is well-stocked with budding young scientists and research students aching to join expeditions into regions where they can satiate their desire to 'find out'; whether they be ornithologists, geologists or ageing lepidopterists. They would have to pay their travel fare, but the food, like the equipment, would come from sponsors. Should the area of research be of a hostile or inaccessible nature, there would be sufficient trained *expéditionnaires* accompanying the scientist-types to ease the difficulties. This then was the idea and, following my earlier Norwegian trips and interest in the glaciers and rivers there, I felt I would start with a journey in the Jotunheim area of central Norway as soon as I left the army.

I felt a personal fascination for the hidden trails, the giant ice-cliffs and the rushing rivers that issue from the glacial gorges, but this in itself was not enough. The days of exploring to discover or to achieve a purely physical goal are numbered: most deserts have been crossed, seas navigated and mountains climbed. Few expeditions nowadays can hope to get off the ground without firm backing of finance and equipment, and this support is not forthcoming unless a sound scientific programme has been worked out so that the objects of the trip are reputable and worthy of the effort and expense involved. With this in mind I made enquiries as to what scientific research was possible in the Jotunheim area, what was already known about its glaciers and ice-caps, and what remained as yet undiscovered or unproven.

When we had last visited the Jotunheim the maps had not seemed sufficiently detailed, so I wrote in the spring of 1970, on my return to England, to Norway's glacier expert Doctor Gunnar Østrem in Oslo. He replied saying that he would very much like to have an accurate survey made of the Fåbergstølsbre, one of the valley glaciers 'flowing' from the Jostedalsbre[1] and at the eastern end of its plateau. Information as to the exact position of the Fåbergstølsbre's tip or 'snout' was urgently required in

1. For the sake of clarity I will use 'Jostedalsbre' to refer to the whole of the central plateau snowfield area. From this central plateau flow twenty-eight main glaciers, the ones which concern the readers of this book are the Bödalsbre, which I had visited in 1967, the Fåbergstølsbre, which we were to survey, and the Briksdalsbre, by which we were to descend.

order to compare its location with that shown on a map made in 1955. Was the glacier receding, growing or moving its course?

The 1955 chart had been made from air photographs taken by the Norwegian authorities, who then flew a second series of photogammetric flights in 1966. By comparing the two resultant maps they had hoped to obtain an accurate idea of the rate of movement of each ice-arm; knowledge of considerable importance to those living in the area. But unfortunately, as Gunnar Østrem explained, there were certain important gaps in the photogammetric charts. The map construction had been based on two flying-lines over the ice-cap and, due to wind conditions, one of these lines did not catch the longest outlet glaciers to the east. The Fåbergstølsbre glacier was the most serious omission and Dr. Østrem stressed that its survey would be of extreme topical interest to his Hydrological and Glaciological Department.

He warned us that this would be no simple task for we would have to tie our section of map in with the trigonometrical points used by the Norwegians in their maps. These points were on high points of the main glacier, towering above the Fåbergstølsbre arm, and they would have to be visited before any survey of the ice-arm could be done. Moreover they were extremely difficult to reach being over six thousand feet above sea-level and rimmed by crevasse-fields. All the necessary survey equipment, delicate theodolites, radios for communication between the various points, bulky poles and tripods, and a hundred other items, would have to be transported on to the plateau top somehow and then moved over the treacherous ice-fields to a position above the Fåbergstølsbre. Sledges and skis would be necessary, as well as tents and food. The only safe track up to the plateau near the Fåbergstølsbre was a difficult route up steep glacial moraines and broken rock for five thousand feet; difficult enough with a small rucksack let alone eight-foot sledges and fifteen-foot marker poles.

The Norwegian authorities naturally had no wish to afford the time, staff, or the money to operate a ground survey of this area, nor indeed another air survey, since it was hardly economic to operate a further photogammetric mission solely for the eastern edge of the vast glacier. With the notorious local mists and blizzards of the Jostedalsbre to confound our theodolite sightings and the difficulty of transporting kit, it seemed the survey would take several weeks to complete.

But then, remembering the parachute jump which had speeded up our last visit to the glaciers, I wrote to Gunnar suggesting that a small team of surveyors might land by helicopter or be parachuted on to the plateau complete with all the necessary equipment.[2] They would not be able to survive for much more than a week on the amount of food they could carry by sledge. But a week should be sufficient for the survey if the team were equipped to live and sleep on the plateau, and so waste no time climbing up to it each time the mists cleared and down again when a blizzard set in. Such a solution might ease the transport and time factors, but it would also add dangers of a different nature. Initial enquiries revealed that a helicopter landing was out of the question – the price would be exorbitant even if we could find a charter company willing to risk a helicopter in the area.

There are many air charter companies operating small aeroplanes in the mountainous region of central Norway at reasonable prices and willing to drop parachutists – at their own risk. Remembering that earlier jump though, I wondered whether it was wise to repeat the performance in so hazardous an area; would we be so lucky with the weather and the soft snow a second time? In 1967 we had had truly perfect conditions over the Jostedalsbre for some five hours, and had made the jump with no wind and not a cloud in the sky. But within a few hours of our landing, high winds had lashed the ice-fields and thick mists obscured the plateau; so we knew well that the climatic moods of the Jostedalsbre could be both changeable and unpredictable. Furthermore, 1967 had been a severe winter with heavy snowfalls; what had the winter of 1969 been like? Would the crevasses lie bare this time?

I wrote to the Tourist Board representative in Loen, the little hamlet in the valley to the north of our earlier dropping zone. The reply came without delay. Flights over the Jostedalsbre had already confirmed that the ice-fields were dangerous this year and

2. As a direct result of the experiences of the Jostedals project, a British scientific expedition in July 1971 parachuted into the Roraima savannah region on the Venezuelan border to speed and facilitate a programme of survey and research.

would of course deteriorate further as the light snow layer covering the ice fissures melted in the summer.

There was, however, a small bowl-shaped depression more or less between two rock formations, the Braeniba and the Lodalskåpa, which was both free of crevasses and somewhat protected from the surface wind currents by the rock outcrops. This crevasse-free area was about one hundred metres square and near to the ice-field where our earlier landing had been made.

To its discredit, this target area lay close to the very edge of the plateau and it would require precise steering on the part of each parachutist to avoid missing the ice-fields altogether and being dashed against the precipice below by the thermal winds that scour the 5,000-foot cliff. But such dangers as these could be anticipated by an expert, so I telephoned Don Hughes at the Netheravon Parachute School and asked him about our chances. He had enjoyed our last expedition and appeared willing to help us again but – not knowing any more than I about survey equipment – could not say whether it would be possible to drop our gear by parachute. He agreed to come with us to supervise the drop, and said that he would train any of our surveyors who were in need of parachute tuition. One thing he was adamant about however. We must go in mid-August or not at all, for calm clear weather would be vital to a safe drop and no other month offered a reasonable chance of good conditions.

Before accepting his offer of help I tried hard to obtain a large helicopter at a reasonable price to avoid the necessity of parachuting. Sir John Walker, an ex-Ambassador in Oslo, succeeded in gaining the permission of the Commander-in-Chief of the Norwegian Air Force to give us helicopter aid if the British Ministry of Defence would sanction our expedition. But the Ministry of Defence were, as is their wont, wary of any expeditions of a non-military nature, and refused – graciously – to give us their blessing.

So we would parachute in with all our equipment.

The use of parachutes in large-scale expeditions had been tried out before but usually only to send in extra food and supplies, not for transporting an entire survey party. In 1935[3] and 1939 the American Geographic sponsored expeditions into the Yukon

3. See *Geographic Review*, 1942 – 'Experiments in Parachuting Supplies'.

mountains. They found that it took four men nine days to transport two weeks' supplies only twelve miles. On the later journey the men took sixteen days to get their supplies to a camp at ten thousand feet. The entire expedition schedules were jeopardised by these time factors until they decided to drop their heavy equipment ahead of them whilst they moved in with the lighter pieces.

Should we succeed on the Jostedalsbre we would be going one better and might set a useful precedent for the future. We would take everything with us. Once descended, it was true, we would have to find our way back to civilisation by normal means but at least half the travelling would be avoided. To persons interested in research work in far-flung regions, such as Greenland, the polar regions or the Andes, economy of effort, time and money is at a premium. By parachuting a well-trained team into or near the designated area, fully equipped for their scientific programme, difficult and dangerous approach marches are avoided.

The Scott Polar Institute showed interest in our idea and in our methods and agreed to help us with survey equipment. Major Blashford-Snell, the chairman of the Scientific Exploration Society, was also extremely interested in the potentials of parachuting into so inhospitable and inaccessible a region as the Jostedals ice-cap and he promised to help us too. He knew the whereabouts and abilities of most of Britain's 'adventurous scientists' and offered to look out for surveyors and scientists for us. He admitted that men who were qualified in these fields and who were also willing to parachute and ski would be few and far between but he promised to search.

Captain Guy Sheridan of the Royal Marines had been in Dhofar with me and with his help I approached the Royal Marines. They promised substantial aid with all climbing and ice equipment.

Marlow Ropes and some sixty other British firms all agreed to help. We would do our best, in return, to test their products under adverse conditions and to boost their sales at home and in Norway through publicity.

At last the expedition was taking shape.

Once the team was on to the ice of the dropping zone the plane would drop supplies and equipment. The men would then have to reach each bundle and collapse the parachutes before the wind caught them and dragged them down a crevasse or over the edge. As soon as everything was assembled kit would be strapped on to sledges and, wearing light langlauf skis, we would drag the sledges to the east where we would pitch a tented camp on the upper rim of the Fåbergstølsbre ice-arm. The amount of weight an eight-man survey team can drag behind skis is limited and that weight must include not only kit but also their food for eight days. All the scientific data would have to be collected and the survey completed in that time.

In order to get all our gear to central Norway we would need Land Rovers. These would have to be driven up to Newcastle, over on the car ferry to Bergen and then on to the aerodrome. Later these Land-Rovers could form a base camp in the valley below the glacier. Those in the base camp would be within reach in case of accident, they would be able to communicate with us by radio as we moved around the plateau and they would be able to co-ordinate all our activities. At a pinch, any scientist who could not parachute could come up from the base camp to do his research, provided he could get his equipment in a rucksack on his back, or we could parachute in with his gear which he could later climb up and fetch. It might also be possible, I thought, for some of the more delicate and expensive survey equipment and scientific data to be taken down the tortuous ravines and moraines on a man's back to the base camp after the survey had been completed. But the bulky poles, 300-foot ropes, tripods, meter staves and tents would have to be lowered down an ice-arm on sledges. This appeared impossible on the heavily crevassed Fåbergstølsbre, for its gradient would not be sufficiently steep to allow sledges to slide over the fissures and so avoid the gaps. Instead the sledges, pushed and pulled by us, were more likely to slide into the fissures. But if the ice-arm we went down was steep enough the sledges might well slide down and clear the chasms through the acute angle of the gradient.

With this in mind I poured over an ancient map of the Jostedalsbre and noticed that a drift trail was shown as running west from the Fåbergstølsbre. It meandered for some forty kilometres through the ice-fields to a glacial arm of unparalleled steepness named the Briksdalsbre, and then continued on down the valley below to the fjords.

All my old fascination in the frozen cattle trails returned. Here was a chance to follow one and at the same time descend by a route which might allow us to lower the sledges with us, avoiding the necessity of abandoning much equipment.

Glancing at a more up-to-date map of the valley below the Briksdalsbre, it was obvious that the ice had retreated considerably. It spilled steeply over the plateau and descended closely contoured cliffs for some three thousand feet to a small lake. There was no road here, so the equipment could not be transferred direct from sledge to Land-Rover. However there was a little road marked which petered out some three miles farther down the valley and a well-marked river ran from the lake down the gorge to the fjords.

I had recently read of an expedition to the cataracts of the Blue Nile Gorge which had succeeded where canoeists had previously failed by using small rubber boats. They had carried much equipment and navigated severe rapids. This information further backed up my hunch that these were just the craft I had long sought for a trans-Norway river journey. At any rate I decided to try to obtain three; one to be parachuted with us uninflated and two to travel with the Land-Rovers, in case the airborne boat went down a crevasse. Whilst we were langlaufing across from the Fåbergstølsbre to the top of the Briksdalsbre, the Land-Rovers would move their base camp to the road below the Briksdalsbre. The two spare boats would then be portaged up the gorge from the base camp by the Land-Rover drivers to the lake at the bottom of the glacier. We would then load the kit off the sledges on to the boats and navigate down the river to the Land-Rovers, or all being well to the sea.

In this way we would bring down and save the heavy equipment, trace a 'drift' trail, descend a glacial arm and with any luck test and prove a suitable craft for navigating Norway's vicious rivers, all in one fell swoop.

Since there were no funds available for three rubber boats or theodolites, all would have to come from British companies who would be willing to loan them in return for what they might gain from advertising the use of their wares on so unusual a venture. This in turn meant trying to arrange contracts for a documentary film and some sort of national newspaper and television network tie-up. My literary agent, George Greenfield, agreed to see what could be done.

It seemed likely as the preparations advanced that the expedition team would number more than a dozen. At least eight men would be needed for a strong survey team. There would be some additional research students, scientists, a doctor, photographer and two or three Land-Rover drivers.

Having consulted the meteorological authorities in Oslo and Bergen, the date for the parachute descent was settled for August 13th and – bearing in mind that the weather must be perfect for the jump – the entire programme was rendered elastic in case we should have to wait for several days for good weather. We would meet in London on August 10th, collect and load the Land-Rovers, and drive to Newcastle to catch the car ferry to Bergen. From Bergen we would drive overnight on the 11th to Loen in the Jotunheim, a small hamlet nestling on the shore of Loenvatnet Lake.

August 12th would be spent on a reconnaissance of the Briksdal glacier and river, and on the 13th, or as soon as the weather was propitious, we would telephone a Bergen air-charter firm for a seaplane. This would land on the lake to collect the survey team and the equipment for the jump. The Land-Rover party were then to drive north-east and over the Grôtli Pass to form a camp below the Fåbergstølsbre.

The survey team must all be capable parachutists and would need to be reliable characters whose participation on a totally voluntary basis would enable them to take part in a unique and testing expedition. Apart from the scientific research they would be carrying out, their reasons for coming must include a personal desire to test themselves against the elements and subjugate their fears and doubts through careful action in potentially unnerving situations. On this point *expéditionnaires* are apt to keep silent, for the public is generally scathing in its reaction to adventures executed for enjoyment and transient personal achievements.

I intended to organise training sessions in the spring in parachuting, 'white water' boating, langlauf ski-ing and climbing to weld the team when it materialised into an efficient body. All would be participating at their own risk but there would always be an element of interdependence, so that each man must be fully versed in the necessary skills.

I visited my literary agent, George Greenfield. He is unique amongst agents in that he specialises in the affairs of Britain's explorers. Not only the small fry like myself but also such men as Francis Chichester, Edmund Hillary and Vivian Fuchs. He has the amazing ability of finding a literary home for almost any worthwhile expedition and his approval of the Norwegian project would set a seal on its financial viability. Great was my relief, one bitter morning in March, when he laid down the carefully prepared expedition prospectus and agreed that he would be able to find newspaper and television sponsors for the venture.

TWO

A Mixed Bag

THE IDEA HAD PROVED FEASIBLE: now for the groundwork. From somewhere in Britain I must find a competent survey team – a minimum of eight persons, all of whom could parachute or were willing to learn how to over the next five months before August. Additionally they must know how to langlauf ski – a skill rarely practised by the British – how to rock climb, and how to control river craft in adverse conditions. Apart from the survey group, there would need to be a biologist, a glaciologist and a geologist. A doctor too, and drivers for the Land-Rovers, must be found, so in early March, whilst working on the Nile book for my publishers, I set about recruiting a suitable crew for the expedition.

Such people were not easy to come by, although I contacted several who initially jumped at the idea but found some excuse to change their minds as soon as funds were mentioned. Individual fares to and from Norway as well as eating expenses must be borne by each man, for there was to be no central fund. Since I explained there would be no division of profits in the unlikely event of expedition expenses being exceeded by T.V. and news coverage fees, there could be no financial incentive to those who volunteered. This worked both ways for there was every likelihood of a substantial loss, and none of the team would be expected to help out in this eventuality.

Most universities have exploration clubs which send out several groups to various climes each year; I intended to visit the major universities to recruit young scientists, but first contacted the five participants of our 1967 expedition. Captain Peter Loyd of the Scots Greys, now flying helicopters in Edinburgh, cast his mind back to that hectic trip, and declined. Nick Holder would be in Sharjah in the Middle East and so unable to come, and Simon Gault was taking his final exams to become a barrister. There remained our 'driver' and 'cook'. Martin Grant-Peterkin was a racing driver and mechanic of expertise who had earlier proved invaluable: he agreed to come again as leader of the Land-Rover party, as did Vanda Allfrey whose camp cooking and dry humour were spicy ingredients for any expedition base. Simon Gault had a Territorial friend in Newcastle named Bob Powell who, as a chartered architect, had completed survey training. The man was a captain in the 17th Battalion of the Parachute Regiment, and a tough pug-nosed rugby player to boot. He sounded suitable so I sent him details of the plan and, having, through his overt enthusiasm, squashed his wife's objections before they were even produced, he 'signed on' with the expedition.

One spring afternoon the rain poured through the dank foliage of Sloane Square's friendly trees, scaring away the pigeons and the daffodil seller with high blood pressure. I stopped taking photos of the fountain and moved off down the King's Road with a newspaper over my head. It struck me how well geared-out for the rain were most of the hippies with their otherwise ridiculous wide-brimmed headgear and all-enveloping cloaks.

A tall semi-hippy in a flared blue suit passed me at speed. I noticed the *Financial Times* under one arm and the well-polished shoes. Hair lay over his coat collar but perhaps, on second thoughts, he looked more like a young executive. He glanced at a shop window and his profile was familiar. Perhaps he sensed my interest, for he turned. It was Johnnie Muir, once a top skier in the army whom I had known in Bavaria years ago. We found a Lyons Corner House and over a coffee discussed our respective activities. Johnnie, it transpired, was bored with London life, with office work and the day to day monotony of accounts. He listened in silence to my ramblings about the Norwegian journey and his eyes glistened as I mentioned my search for personnel.

He would love to come, he said, if only he could parachute. Some fifty yards down the road was the Territorial Centre of various Parachute Regiments and after a talk to a sergeant there, Johnnie had his parachute tuition fully arranged. Unfortunately all did not go well with his training over the next three months as he later told me. His first weekend visit to Netheravon coincided with strong winds so the instructors had him jumping off high benches on to supposedly soft mats to teach him to tuck in his long ungainly limbs and 'roll, not collapse!' on hitting the ground. Johnnie was black and blue by the end of the weekend but determined to carry on. He had better luck the next time for, with blue skies and a light breeze, he managed two jumps from a de Havilland Rapide. The first time, he admitted, he hit the ground like the proverbial sack of potatoes – forgetting all he had been taught the weekend before – but he had done it; he had jumped and was still alive!

Next time the wind caught him too high and, making a basic error, Johnnie steered in entirely the wrong direction to find himself descending with speed towards a group of council houses surrounded by a network of telephone wires and power lines.

With a frozen grin of impotent anticipation, quite unable to think of anything, let alone the emergency drills he had been taught, he awaited the worst. He had heard the grizzly tales of instructors; how former pupils had ended as deep fried shish-kebab on high-load electricity lines. But Johnnie's luck was in. He missed the lines, skimmed over a roof by a hair's breadth, and touched down in a vegetable patch. The occupants of the house had been having tea and were sipping from their cups as they stood watching Johnnie pick himself from the crushed cabbages. He declined their kind offer to join them for tea and began the tiring walk back to the hangar with his heavy parachutes. But still he was progressing: he must polish up on his steering next time and all would be well.

His third brave attempt was his last for he chose a windy day and came down heavily backwards, dislocating his thumb and completely confirming his already growing fears that if the grassy fields of Netheravon produced such horrors, how much worse would be a 6,000-foot ice-patch surrounded by cliffs. His decision to drop out of the para-survey team coincided with news from Martin Grant-Peterkin that he had become adjutant of the Royal Scots Greys and his leave was postponed. Johnnie agreed to take his place as Road Party leader.

Checking up in the *Daily Telegraph Magazine* about the behaviour of rubber boats on the Blue Nile Gorge Expedition I decided it might be worth contacting their boat party leader, an army captain named Roger Chapman. He had received an M.B.E. for bravery during that journey and his knowledge of navigating rough rivers in small boats must be unrivalled. He turned out to be studying geography at Oxford University, where I visited him and told him of the expedition and its need to return to civilisation via the Briksdal gorge. My mention of rough water probably decided him, though he was also a keen parachutist, a langlauf skier and a qualified surveyor. The expedition appeared to have been moulded to his taste and he telephoned later that month to say he would come.

The team was growing and, at home in Sussex, British Rail lorries were daily getting themselves wedged in our narrow-walled approach lane bringing crates of food or equipment from sponsor companies. Enough Wrigley's chewing gum for a regiment in Vietnam, soups, dehydrated vegetables and – everywhere one looked – baked beans. Specially packed dehydrated assault rations too had arrived from the War Office for evaluation: these were sufficiently light and highly calorised for one man to carry four days' food on his back whilst on the glacier.

The Rover Company, as a result of the publicity afforded them during the Nile Hovercraft Expedition, had written to say they would lend us three Land-Rovers for a month. This was excellent news, for my earlier enquiries had met with the reply that over two thousand such requests came to Rover's annually and a ruling had reluctantly been made against any assistance to expeditions.

The Avon Rubber Company had loaned boats for the navigation of the Blue Nile, two of which were now in my possession, and a promise of another specially modified craft assured us a reasonable chance of descending the cataracts of the Briksdalsbre.

A letter arrived from Australia in early March from Patrick Brook who had been my adjutant in the Muscat Regiment during the 1969 campaign against the Dhofari communist guerrillas. He was coming back to his regiment in England and would like to join the expedition in August if he could. He was an experienced langlaufer and there was little he did not know about radios. This decided me, for we would be taking some sixteen radios on the expedition and would need an expert. Without good communications between the scattered survey groups, the ice-camp, and the base party, we could not hope to complete the work in a week. Patrick appeared on first acquaintance to be quite incapable of exertion. He was a self-confessed gourmet whose main delights were large breakfasts eaten in total silence apart from the rustle of newspapers, professionally conducted games of roulette, poker and backgammon, and a well-stocked supply of the better brands of whisky. But I had seen Patrick coming back from an operation in Dhofar with a bullet through his arm and his hip-radio smashed by another. His patrol had been marching for twelve hours through extremes of climate and terrain, carrying their dead and wounded and in permanent danger of being cut off from their base. Patrick was as cool as a cucumber when he got back and, after a double whisky and a good sleep, he refused to fly back to Salalah for sick leave. He could not parachute but promised to learn before August.

Two of the team, it was discovered, were unable to langlauf ski so, early in April, a weekend course near Aviemore was arranged on their behalf to teach them the rudiments of this difficult sport which entails a movement rather like skating on skis. Only the toecap of a skier's boot is fixed to either ski leaving the rest of the foot free to move. Since mists covered the slopes and driving sleet made visibility poor, conditions were not ideal for instruction. Both pupils spent the weekend running into each others' backsides in the gloom and wading through the drifts searching for runaway skis. However, since both were reasonably adept on the normal downhill type of ski, they would no doubt get the knack soon enough on the glaciers.

At this time I visited the B.B.C.2 studios with Bob King who owned a flourishing film distribution company, and had helped over the filming of a previous expedition. The B.B.C. men liked the Norwegian idea and advised us to go ahead with a documentary film and bring them the finished work for evaluation after the expedition. This was all very well. If they bought the film, they would have risked nothing but, if they didn't, Bob King stood to lose a packet. However, he found a photographer for us, Norwegian-born Egil Woxholt who had directed the ski-ing and underwater sequences for the latest James Bond film, and saw opportunities for an 'action-packed documentary' so long as we could find a helicopter for him to film from! Had we been able to afford one, I explained, we would hardly be parachuting on to the glacier top.

Bob King was still trying to recover the considerable loss incurred by our Nile hovercraft film and much of my time that spring was spent in a church vestry in Lombard Street where we had fitted out an editing studio in which to finish off the edited version of the film. Knee-deep in snaking coils of celluloid one lunchtime, I heard the Rector shout from below announcing a visitor. Wondering who had traced me to this far-fetched lair, I went next door where maps of Norway lined the walls and photos of the Jostedals Glacier littered the tables. A very large fellow with a green spotted bow-tie appeared and clenched my hand in a knuckle-crushing grip which left it numb for several minutes.

'Brendan O'Brien,' he announced, 'pleased to meet you. Major John Blashford-Snell of the Scientific Exploration Society sent me here as you need a biologist for your Norwegian Expedition.'

As I digested this he added that he could climb on rock and ice, and was extremely interested in the insect life of the glaciers. I was unaware that there were any insects on the Jostedalsbre but he explained they were microscopic and little research had been carried out hitherto on their nature. He appeared to be a pillar of strength and activity and determined to join us.

Our glaciologist was not so easy to find and not till late the following June did Roger Chapman contact the Scott Polar Institute in Cambridge to find a volunteer named Norris Riley. Norris was a perfectionist and an outdoor man who loved the world of ice. He had just returned from two years at the British Antarctic Base in Halley Bay and we arranged for him to join a UNESCO glaciology course in Sweden which would bring him right up to date on Norwegian glacier research.

When we had reached Wadi Halfa in the Nubian Desert during the hovercraft journey the year before, the expedition

(Roger Chapman) One of the second 'stick' leaves the Cessna over the glacier without mishap.

Some of the 'team' at Bergen. *From left to right:* Ranulph Fiennes, Bob Powell, Roger Chapman, Johnnie Muir, David Murray-Wells, Brendan O'Brien, Peter Booth, Gillie Kennard, Henrik Forss.

The sledge journey from the Dropping Zone to Ice Camp.

photographer had been badly burnt. We had had morphine and paraffin gauze but no doctor. Once bitten, twice shy – I had resolved to participate in no further trips without a doctor going too. After many fruitless telephone calls and letters I gave up trying to find a British doctor who could parachute and ski, and wrote to a Finn named Doctor Henrik Forss who had already accompanied British expeditions in the Middle East and was at home on skis having spent many months in Arctic Lappland with sledging teams. Henrik agreed to meet us in Norway without asking any further questions as to our schedule and intentions.

George Greenfield took me to have lunch with the editor of the *Sunday Mirror* but the *Mirror* was having difficulty with its weekend magazine which shortly afterwards collapsed and was a financial fiasco. We tried the *Daily Telegraph* next. Their magazine editor, John Anstey, came to lunch and agreed to draw up a contract to cover the Norwegian expedition by sending a photographer and a writer with us. This would put our numbers up to seventeen persons and three Land-Rovers, so it was as well the Bergen Shipping Line were lowering their transport fares considerably for us.

A young geologist named Peter Booth telephoned from Leeds University to ask about North Africa and the difficulties of overland travel there. He was planning to drive along the Nile-side tracks, roughly following the route of our hovercraft journey, and sounded an ambitious type. We met in London the next week and Peter agreed to shelve his North African trip and come to Norway instead. Since he could not parachute but lived right next door to Netheravon Parachute School, he resolved to learn as soon as the University spring term was ended. All these volunteers came from different parts of the country, few of them could parachute, some could not ski or climb and all of us, except Roger Chapman, were ignorant of the little-known skill of manoeuvring rubber boats in raging torrents. By August everyone must be more than just proficient at all these things, for their lives and the lives of the others would depend on their skill. This was not being melodramatic, simply realistic. Risks foreseen and catered for were no longer risks and if, like good drivers, we expected the unexpected, we must train accordingly. With this in mind, a programme was planned stretching from March until August.

A river of similar conditions to those anticipated in Norway must be found somewhere in Britain where Roger could teach the team to control the rubber boats no matter how rough the conditions or whether the boat was moving sideways, backwards or, as after a capsize, upside down. Before he left Britain for the Blue Nile journey he had taken two of the rubber boats to the River Dee near Llangollen in Wales. There is a half-mile series of small rapids there which provides excellent fishing at expensive rates, and serves as a reasonably unnerving 'beginner's slope' for those learning to control the Avon boats.

One frosty day in early April, a battered collection of cars arrived outside the Territorial Barracks in Wrexham and for the first time the various members of the expedition met one another. They slept in a dormitory and fed on tinned food prepared by Vanda Allfrey who had also arrived to 'inspect' the team. Some were quiet and careful to let out little about themselves and their personalities, others were boisterous and eager to show themselves to be up to whatever action lay in store.

To begin with there were slide shows showing the Jostedal area and the grand scale of the problems to be faced. There were discussions on the use of the equipment, the radios and the sledges, and a nine hours' 'refresher' course was given on the methods of survey to be used to chart the inaccessible Fåbergstølsbre. Theodolites of a new and robust design had been loaned us which might withstand the shock of a parachute drop: even the more practised of our surveyors would need bringing up to date on these precision instruments.

Then on the Sunday morning – not long after dawn – the team was assembled on the wet grass of the guard-room lawn wearing frogman suits, life jackets and fibreglass helmets. Long rope-cutting knives were strapped to their calves.

Two Redshank boats lay side by side on the grass, each as long and as wide as, say, a Land-Rover but light enough to be carried on the heads of its crew of three. Each member of the crew wields a single-bladed paddle, two men seated side by side in the centre and the 'skipper' wedged into the narrow rear compartment, so that by applying all his weight to his paddle, and using it much like a rudder, he can steer with finesse. We were planning to go where no canoeist would venture, for metal or fibreglass, however skilfully controlled, would be no match for the tremendous weight of water which pours tortuously through and over the boulders of the Briksdal gorge. The rubberoid floors of our craft had already been thickened with a Neoprene layer which no rock might pierce. There were thin floorboards too, but these were only to protect our kneecaps from injury as sharp rocks thudded against the hull. Further modifications were a veritable rash of canvas handgrips sewn into the inside of the boat, into the inflated walls and even into the length and breadth of the hull lining. This meant that, on capsizing in rapids, the crew could climb on to the upturned craft and, grasping the handgrips, cling to them until calmer waters allowed time to re-right the boat. The three paddles were tied by short lengths of cording to the inflated ring so they would not be easily lost. It struck me how easily all these straps and loose cords might entwine one's limbs in rough water and drag a body beneath the craft.

Roger had already been through the cataracts of the Blue Nile in these two little boats – named Faith and Charity – and was confident of their functional toughness. He divided the team into three-man crews and the dry training commenced. Rehearsing capsize drills on grass would no doubt have been hilarious but Roger was taking us to the Snake's Tail rapids later in the day, so we took the practice seriously, each crew attempting to achieve faster times than the other.

Perspiring freely in the rubber suit, I was in the midst of the re-righting phase when an odd incident occurred. Amusing at the time, it was later to be remembered when a similar event caused a serious accident in Norway.

The three of us in Charity had just rolled from the grassy 'river' back into our re-righted craft and were frantically searching for our respective paddles. Mine was trapped beneath the boat. Levering it out I found its retaining cord was snared around something and so pulled it as hard as I might. It gave slightly but still snagged. I tugged at it viciously, and then sensed more than heard a strangled grunt from my next-door crewman, Brendan O'Brien, the biologist; glancing over my shoulder I noticed that his hands were clawing his neck, his face a mottled puce, and his tongue thrust full out from his mouth. It took a little while to realise the cause of his plight, but on looking closer I saw that the thin sharp cord from my paddle had twined itself under a davit and round his neck, and was throttling him. I released him with alacrity and he went off to recover. The training went on.

The River Dee was cold for there was frost on the ground but we stayed until dusk, experiencing for the first time the exhilarating feel of a Redshank shuddering under the impact of curling, rushing waves; the roaring sound of approaching rapids rushing to meet the little craft, threatening to envelop it and cover its occupants; the sudden panic when mistimed steering took us hurtling sideways into a boulder and we cowered on the floor for fear of our skulls rattling along the rocky overhang of a sharp bend. Shaken but elated we listened to Roger's closing advice.

'That was an amazingly useless effort. You must all realise that the Dee is a millpond compared with what you will face next August. You must pull your fingers out and get this steering mastered, otherwise there will be trouble in Norway. The steersmen must really fight the water to get the right angle of approach; it's no good just dipping your paddles in the water from time to time . . . if the front men cannot keep up the forward motion of the craft you can't expect any steering response.'

We came to the Snake's Tail again in April and finding the water too low moved our attentions to Llangollen Weir and to Chester. Soon we were proficient and confident that we could steer the little boats through anything Norway's cataracts might offer, whether we capsized or not. The boats were sent back to Avon's Llanelli factory for further modifications: a Neoprene lining was added to their upper sides so that they became as tough when capsized as otherwise.

Another member of the team, and leader of our survey programme, was Captain Geoffrey Holder, a brilliant engineer and one of Britain's leading free-fall parachutists. He knew that a documentary film was to be made of the expedition and, having experienced the total inability of most photographers to record the split-seconds of action during a jump, urged me to invite our cinematograph man to Netheravon to experience the difficulties of filming one plane from another when both are falling and rising unpredictably in air pockets.

Geoff completed a final analysis of the survey programme towards the end of June and decided we were understaffed. Another man was required, but this was difficult at so late a stage and we were lucky to find a young student from Yorkshire with parachuting experience: David Murray-Wells was twenty-one years old and the youngest member of the team.

Throughout the spring, the team had been learning to free-fall individually at parachute schools all over Britain, but in July Don Hughes decided to centralise the training at Netheravon where the survey team might learn to drop as a group, to trust one another and to develop an efficient mode of leaving the plane one after another with minimal time-lag between each man. A couple of seconds gap between two parachutists leaving the aircraft could mean many yards distance between them on landing. In Norway, where the safe dropping zone would be no more than two hundred square metres, the team must drop as close to one another as possible.

I had heard from Westwing Air Charter Company in Bergen that they would provide us with a small Cessna seaplane for the jump. This was the only available plane for the venture. On our earlier jump, in 1967, Westwing had flown us over the glacier in a large Otter seaplane with an excellent pilot. Unfortunately the Otter had recently crashed in the Norwegian mountains and the pilot had been killed.

The little Cessna would take, Don estimated, at least four flights from the lake to deliver all the team and equipment on to the ice. However, there were no alternative machines and Westwing's terms were extremely generous.

We spent long hours telephoning and writing to find a Cessna aeroplane from which we could practice in England. There were simply none available and we would have to make do with thorough practice from the Rapide planes at Netheravon. When we reached Norway, we would just have to adapt our ejection position to suit the different structure of the Cessna seaplane with its metal floats.

Patrick Brook had been summoned to Belfast where the Irish terrorists were being troublesome. He wrote to say that he had located a parachute school near Belfast but that since the weather was permanently foul, he had not yet managed to jump. He had also been somewhat put off by the story of a guardsman who had parachuted there on a recent exercise. His parachute had not opened properly and he had failed to pull his reserve 'chute handle until the very last moment so that he hit the ground virtually unchecked and head first. A dropping zone official rushed over to find the collapsed canopy but no guardsman. Then he noticed a large pair of army boots upside down and protruding from a little black peat-bog, so glutinous and slimy that the guardsman had performed a neat dive into its maw without breaking a bone in his body. They pulled him out and, washing out his nostrils, breathed the life back into him. Patrick swore to the truth of this tale, and all the instructors at Netheravon had heard it, but then there are, and always will be, some amazing stories attached to an activity as emotion-packed as parachuting.

Peter Booth, the geologist, was also lagging behind the others in proficiency. Each beginner is initially made to leave the aircraft in the prescribed free-fall position but instead of his pulling a rip-cord, there is a static line from the fuselage to his parachute pack which opens his 'chute automatically as he falls away from the plane. When he has left the wing correctly in this fashion several times, he must, on counting to three, reach his arms across and tug open a dummy rip-cord – watched from above and below by instructors. Eventually, when he has developed self-confidence and a good falling position, he will be allowed to jump without a static line, falling for five seconds before pulling his rip-cord.

Peter had reached this last stage without trouble but thereafter some small lack of symmetry in his falling position made his body aerodynamically unsound and, every time he jumped, he performed an alarming series of aerial gymnastics which usually resulted in his having to pull his rip-cord prematurely. Don became worried and Peter was put back to static line jumps. He came to me one morning in late July and, in threatening tones, warned me not to remove him from the team. He knew he would be all right, he said, before we left for Norway. He was a brave man, I thought, feeling sure that I would leave parachuting well alone if my body started behaving as his did when airborne.

Our earlier photographer, Egil Woxholt, who had recorded much of the white water training on the Dee, had succumbed to a tempting offer to direct a major film in India and the expedition was now to be covered by Independent Television News. Their ciné man arrived at Netheravon one weekend in early August full of imaginative ideas on free-fall photography although he had not actually filmed any jumping before. It was a cloudy day with a fair amount of wind about and we circled many times waiting for a gap in the clouds with a Cessna attempting to keep alongside us so that the I.T.N. man was well lined up when we jumped. Alas! he was badly airsick, longing to get his feet back on terra firma, and quite unable to get any reasonable film by the time the weather cleared and eight of our team plunged through the air in our final rehearsal for Norway. By way of encouragement as we regrouped in the hangar for de-briefing our sergeant instructor harangued us,

'Thank God I'm not responsible for you's lot in Norway or wherever it is that you're off to. Never in twelve years of instruction have I seen such a collective abortion as your last effort.'

The team was now complete and well prepared for the hazards which lay ahead, but there were technical problems still unsolved. At Netheravon Don Hughes and Geoff spent long hours working out the weight and density of the equipment bundles: some six hundred kilos of bulky equipment including sledges, long metal survey poles, delicate radios and theodolites, subtense bars and sledge hammers, all to be evenly packed to certain rigid specifications before they could be safely parachuted.

Roger Chapman tucked himself away at the Army School of Survey and corresponded further with Dr. Gunnar Østrem at the Hydrological Department of the Oslo Electricity Board. The Scott Polar Institute and the Oxford School of Geodosy were also helpful, but problems arose when the Norwegian authorities refused to send us the co-ordinate figures of their national grid system without which we could not accurately relate our charts to any existing maps. After three months of correspondence with the Foreign Office they relented and the vital figures arrived.

Two days before we were due to leave Britain, Johnnie Muir and his road party drove the three Land-Rovers from the Rover Company's London centre to my mother's house in Sussex where the sitting-room had been converted into a storeroom. Some three thousand items, nearly all of which had been donated by British firms, were loaded inside or on to roof-racks of the vehicles. Possibly the strangest of the crates was that containing soaps, deodorants, shampoos and shaving lotions – a gift from Yardleys.

Since there were no financial sponsors at all to the expedition it was as well the food and equipment companies had been so generous. I remembered with a shudder my very first expedition over ten years ago when some £80 was lacking to buy a two-seater canoe in which to cross Norway from Bergen to Oslo. The summer holidays began and the Southdown Bus Company agreed to employ me cleaning their double-deckers from four until eleven a.m. every morning at their Midhurst depot. I lived near Cowdray Park some three miles from Midhurst and so took a bus home for lunch. At two o'clock each day our next-door neighbour, a keen polo player, paid me to deliver three of his ponies to the polo ground near Midhurst. Riding one and leading the other two through the rolling fields of the Park, I would hand them over to the grooms and walk past the ruined castle to Midhurst's Angel Hotel. Here, five hours of dish washing was remunerative and ended with a large free meal selected from the day's menu. A quick sleep at a cousin's antique shop and then back to the bus washing. After a month £80 – and the canoe – were mine but a cruel fate intervened.

Over the preceding years, in the company of some village friends, we had excavated a large cave, close to my mother's house, by burrowing into the side of a nearby slope. The result was a well-concealed hideout or 'fall-out shelter' as we termed it, which we enlarged from time to time and propped up with timbers. Although it was entirely hidden from view the cavity stretched beneath one of Lord Cowdray's arable fields. That summer the field was to be ploughed and great was the surprise and horror of the tractor driver when the ground beneath his vehicle gave way without warning and totally swallowed both the tractor and plough. Lord Cowdray's estate agent informed the local policeman who, without hesitation, visited my mother. A large bill was sent to me, and only by selling the hard earned canoe could I pay it in full.

On August 10th the team assembled at a flat near Sloane Square. Looking at them I wondered if all would be returning at the end of the month. We had just heard the news of a fatal accident on the Anapurna South Face Expedition, and memories of another death by drowning during the Blue Nile venture still niggled me. Ice and rapids – both are potential killers unless one pays them sufficient respect, and this we intended to do to the best of our recently acquired ability.

THREE

Race Against The Clouds

BEFORE DAWN ON August 11th the three Land-Rovers sped up the M1, packed to the gunwales, with the red and white survey flags fluttering like so much bunting from their poles high on the roof-racks. There were sixteen members of the expedition on their way to Newcastle but it was difficult to spot their whereabouts in the heavily laden vehicles. All, except presumably the drivers, were fast asleep recovering from the exertions of the previous night's celebrations. The wind blew strong and the wind blew high, and the little convoy jigged up the central carriageway. A pair of boots was pressed against a rear window pane: Peter Booth, wedged between the roof and a layer of stacked parachutes, lay snoring his way northwards, dreaming no doubt of a geologist's paradise high in the Norwegian peaks.

The highly complicated diversion system at the southern approaches to Newcastle was then an interwoven series of badly signed roundabouts as the new roads took shape. Even before reaching the swing bridge over the Tyne I was surprised to find myself passing the other two Land-Rovers which had quite definitely been behind me on the motorway. When this happened a second time, I realised there must be something seriously wrong with the road signs or my interpretation of them. My navigator was fast asleep, his adenoids rattling down by the dashboard, so I glanced at a compass, headed north ignoring the road signs and soon arrived at the greasy Tyne.

Bob Powell lived at Gosforth in the northern outskirts of the city and we invaded his kitchen for a giant-size brunch before driving down to the docks. Bob's wife kindly drove me to another part of the city suburbs in her car whilst the others dug into their gargantuan grill.

I had received a letter from my ex-fiancée the day before saying she might be coming down from the north-west of Scotland and would meet me at a mutual friend's house in Newcastle. I had known her for fourteen years on and off, and we had been engaged for two years before circumstances – mainly my unfortunate addiction to wandering – had made us break things off that April.

Now she was working for the National Trust for Scotland in faraway Torridon and aqualung diving for scallops in the sea lochs in her spare time.

She arrived in Newcastle just before we caught the boat and, on seeing her after so long, I knew there could be no other – as the saying goes – and so asked her to marry me as soon as we returned from the expedition. She agreed, but later reflected that her affirmative reply was only due to the thoughts that she knew would otherwise haunt her should I end up refrigerated in a crevasse.

Our boat, the S.S. *Leda*, left the Tyne Commission Quay at midday and we were on our way, the subconscious thrill of anticipation at what was to come already gnawing at the pits of our stomachs. The North Sea was in a rare good mood and the ships' liberal supply of paper baskets was not in the usual heavy demand. There was dancing on board and an adequate sprinkling of fair Scandinavian wenches in Norwegian sweaters and mini-skirts. But the expedition members, for the most part, were single-minded, and many hours were spent practising with the four different types of radio down in the bowels of the ship.

Some of the team sat at the bar licking one thousand five hundred stamps and sticking them to specially printed Expedition Commemoration envelopes which would later be sold to European and American philatelists. There were two hundred and fifty sets each consisting of six envelopes. Each envelope would have a Norwegian stamp and at six stages of the journey – at such places as Bergen or Loen – we would have one envelope from each set stamped by the local postmaster, but it would not actually be posted. All the sets would be returned to a philatelic agent in London on our arrival back in England – one of the many activities which helped to meet the expedition costs.

Towards midnight the *Leda* began to roll unevenly: the licking operations became fitful and were soon abandoned altogether. Don Hughes and Geoff gravitated to the bar and spent the entire crossing sampling the various brands of Danish lager. One of our reserved bunks was still vacant; Alex Lowe, the photographer assigned to the expedition by the *Telegraph Magazine*, had not turned up. Still, we were all armed with cameras and he might well fly direct to meet us in Bergen.

The following morning I joined Geoff and Don at the bar. Knowing that there would be little enough time for last-minute arrangements once we arrived in Bergen, I discussed the parachute jump with Don who would remain with the Westwing pilot when the rest of us drove to Loen. Whilst he waited in Bergen he would work out the weight and dimensions of bundles portable on the floats of the Cessna. Don reflected that we would be lucky indeed should we get the clear sky and low windspeeds which had made everything so easy in 1967.

'It's far more likely that the winds and low cloudbase will make it impossible to jump on the 13th,' Don mused. 'The Bergen area has the highest rainfall quota in Europe and the Jostedal spends three-quarters of any year swathed in local mist; never mind the cloudbase. What happens if we get nil visibility above the glacier on the 13th, 14th and 15th and maybe for the rest of the week? You will have to postpone the survey indefinitely, because I'm certainly not letting anyone jump in bad conditions.'

'We can't postpone the survey programme for more than three days,' I replied, 'since it too is impossible to execute in misty conditions. Without the triangulation point sightings to establish the initial control points, we won't be able to start, so we must get clear weather. Geoff and Bob have to be back home by the end of August, so, looking at the schedule backwards . . . we will just have to jump by the 15th even if the winds are a little over the safety limit.'

But Don was adamant.

'You know I'll stretch a point if I can – otherwise I wouldn't be here – but it would be sheer lunacy to attempt the jump if the winds get up. If anyone gets into trouble, pulls too early, and gets blown just a few hundred yards too far, I wouldn't like to answer for the consequences. There's sheer black rock dropping away for four thousand feet, with thermal wind currents scouring the gullies. Get caught in one of those and you'll be dashed against the rock. There are down-draughts too which would deflate a canopy and you'd find yourself free-falling again. I'm not being pessimistic, you know, just realistic. If you were all experts, we might chance the conditions slightly, but you're not much better than beginners. So I'm afraid it's a question of good weather and not much wind, or we don't jump.'

I could visualise what would happen to Don – as head of Britain's leading parachute school – should he drop us in conditions acknowledged to be unsafe; if one or all of us were to crack our skulls against the crags surrounding the dropping zone. His was the ultimate responsibility and therefore the decision to jump or not to jump lay in his very capable hands. So I stopped pressing the point and made a mental note to pray hard for clement weather on the 13th.

There was no point in formulating alteranative plans since there would be no way of surveying the Fåbergstølsbre without getting the team – and a large amount of heavy equipment – on to the 6,000-foot plateau. It had seemed so simple in theory to drop everything and everyone on to the top. But now, as the day of reckoning approached, a series of 'ifs' and 'buts' were raising their ugly heads.

Perhaps we could drop all the equipment on to the plateau and hire a guide to lead us up the precipitous cliff paths unencumbered by heavy kit. But, as Geoff pointed out, we would stand a strong chance of losing the parachuted bundles unless there was a carefully positioned cordon around the dropping zone waiting to receive them. The equipment might well go wide, for after all the parachutes could not be steered once the bundles left the aeroplane. Even if they landed in roughly the right area, the 'chutes would quickly have to be collapsed before the wind caught them and dragged the bundles over the ice and away.

To climb up would take us a day or more, during which time the weather might change so that a kit drop would be impossible. Then we would look foolish: a survey party with no theodolites, no radios and no sledges for the remainder of the heavy gear.

The expense of hiring a seaplane for a day was exorbitant too. Once we started separating ourselves from our kit and keeping the machine hanging around whilst we climbed and the weather deteriorated, charter prices would soar. A helicopter, double the expense of a plane, would not have sufficient fuel capacity to complete the flying hours required to transport such a weight of men and equipment, unless it returned to its base to refuel. This too would be economically beyond our scope.

Geoff, who had not commented on the more obvious problems, now suggested another potential fly in the ointment.

'As Don hasn't seen the Cessna yet and has no idea of the size or strength of its floats, there's no certainty that we can drop some of the weightier bundles at all. Two things could happen and either would be disastrous to the Cessna. The bundles containing the sledges, skis and bamboo survey poles, for instance, are over eight feet long and three feet wide, but they're not all that heavy. When Don looses the retaining straps securing them to a float they might not necessarily fall away as expected and activate their static lines in the normal way.'

Geoff took a gulp of lager with obvious relish.

'It is just as much on the cards that they tilt and rotate in the first grip of the slipstream. Then they would tear away the tailplane or float rudder like so much papier mâché. That would please the pilot. The other thing – and this could happen just as easily with the bulky bundles of rations, rucksacks or radios – is the possibility of a static line deploying too near a float and snagging one of the rudder lines. That too would be critical damage, though not evident until the pilot next tried to land!'

Geoff and Don had both witnessed serious parachuting accidents, usually caused by a moment's carelessness; but new equipment, an unsuitable aeroplane and a virgin dropping zone were a lethal combination which could lead to a mishap however much care was taken. They had no delusions about this and I was grateful to them for the risks they would be running on behalf of the expedition; in particular Don who, long after the rest of us were – one hoped – safely down on the ice, would be wedged in the doorway by the slipstream heaving weighty packs into the void in the knowledge that a slightly mistimed push would cripple the aeroplane.

I digested these last-minute warnings from the professionals with gravity; but none of us could predict the event which was to go within an ace of causing disaster for it was as unavoidable as it was unforeseen.

The S.S. *Leda* had not stopped at Stavanger so we came to Bergen shortly before midday on August 11th. As soon as the gangway was down, a jostling bevvy of journalists and T.V. men came aboard. A tall man who followed a short distance behind them subjected us to a careful scrutiny as we lined the ship's railings to savour the briny atmosphere of fish and diesel. He spotted Roger and his stern face crinkled with the pleasure of seeing an old friend. They exchanged greetings and Roger introduced us. This was Doctor Henrik Forss, one of Sweden's most eminent research physicians. He looks in his early thirties but is forty and attributes his fitness to the yoga and karate camps which he attends annually. This was not the first British expedition he had accompanied as field medico, but as he laughingly admitted it was the most likely to require his services before its completion.

Since he had spent many days in the Finnish Arctic with sledging expeditions, he knew more about the vagaries and dangers of ice than the rest of us, and was a vital addition to our team. He was a Finn by origin but had spent little time in his native land. He had recently visited the North Vietnamese and sheltered from U.S. bombing raids whilst tending wounded civilians. His stories of adventure in the Congo and Libya would make an arresting book. He was also a specialist in child psychology and rehabilitation with artificial limbs.

Henrik was of European outlook and happily donned the orange anorak of the expedition with its shoulder-mounted Union Jack.

The *Leda*'s steward was fussing unintelligibly and Henrik demonstrated his first and most obvious talent by translating: we were all required in the first-class bar for the press conference.

We arrived to find the press assembled around a conference table drinking at the expense of the Bergen Line with their notebooks and tape recorders at the ready. T.V. cameras whirred as we squeezed on to a long settee, recording too the mammoth posters on the wall behind us – pinned there by Vanda and Rosch, the expedition secretaries – which depicted the new Range-Rover vehicle in all its glory and some Avon boats descending rapids on the Blue Nile.

The proposed jump on to the glacier was of major interest in Norway as we soon discovered, but there were some points about which the press were very curious.

'Why,' asked a rabbity creature with reflecting dark glasses, 'were we surveying a glacier which had already been adequately mapped by the Norwegian authorities?' 'Why were we landing by parachute above the glacier instead of climbing it or even landing by helicopter?' They seemed satisfied by our straight-forward answers and when they discovered our doctor was a Scandinavian, barraged him with a number of further queries which they had presumably found difficult to phrase in English.

'Why, after completing our scientific work, did we intend to cross to the northern flank of the glacier and descend via the perilous Briksdalsbre and the glacial river that issues from it? Why not come down one of the recognised routes using local guides?'

Henrik, well versed as to the background and motives of the expedition, explained that with heavy laden sledges and rucksacks it was considerably easier to lower equipment down a 3,000-foot ice-face than to manhaul it item by item, down a slippery rock path which at times would deteriorate into a crumbling ledge. Our route would, if all went well, enable us to descend all the way to a motorable road without man-handling the heavy kit. It would be transferred from the sledges into the Avon boats when we reached the Briksdal lake and then, after a four- or five-mile paddle down the gorge, we could unload everything straight into the Land-Rovers. The use of gravity not manpower was to be the key to our transport problems.

The conference broke up: and three of the reporters warned us that they would be chartering planes from which to photograph the jump on the 13th.

The Land-Rovers drove through the customs without problem.

There were some three thousand meticulously packed items in, on and behind the three vehicles and any official who contemplated searching them would certainly be late home that evening. After Henrik and his bags were crammed in, there was no room left in any of the Rovers.

A heavily-built cinephotographer then arrived with an array of cameras and suitcases. He introduced himself as John Collins from Independent Television News. He had just flown from the riots in Belfast to cover the parachute jump and wanted to come to Loen with us. There just wasn't room, so we hired a trailer locally to hitch behind a Land-Rover and reserved a bunk on a coastal steamer which would take John Collins to somewhere quite near Loen during the night. Then he mentioned his expense account: food was quite excellent on these coastal boats, so, why not one of us accompany him? Patrick Brook appeared as from nowhere at the mention of *haute cuisine* and the two of them left us to spend the night in an orgy of gastronomic experiments on board some comfortable tug whilst we jolted round hairpin bends for nine cramped hours.

I remembered Patrick's last free feast which had lasted for eight days.

Six of us had landed in Bahrein awaiting a plane to Muscat where we were due to join the Sultan's Armed Forces. However, the day we arrived there, the pilots went on strike so we were stranded.

Since the Sultan was now our employer, Patrick argued, he must presumably be paying for our upkeep. This summary of the financial situation was for him the beginning of a prolonged exploration into the many and varied delicacies which the plush hotels of the island had to offer – all at an exorbitant price.

The pilot's strike lasted eight days, so that Patrick was grossly gorged by the time we eventually emplaned for Muscat. He was greeted, on arrival, by temperatures of over 110 degrees in the shade and the news that he must immediately get ready for a drive of some six hundred miles through the desert to join his company in Dhofar. He was looking quite green as his open Land-Rover roared off into the leaden heat.

The occasion had a moral, though it had obviously not taught Patrick a lesson.

During the tacheometric work on the Fåbergstolsnøse . . ., Roger tries to 'level the bubbles' in a high wind.

Geoff and David at the eastern Control Point separated from the main glacier and observing the flowing tongue of the Fåbergstølsbre.

Survey work on the Fåbergstølsbre.

The survey team during the tacheometric work on the Fåbergstølsbre negotiating the ice.

That night as his vehicle bumped through the soft sand of the southern deserts, he slumped groaning in the passenger seat. Racked by nightmarish visions of broiled sheep's eye, prawn cocktails and oily shish-kebab, Patrick nodded off to sleep and soon his limp snoring body fell from the doorless vehicle into the sand. Woken smartly, he found himself in the choking cloud of dust set up by his vehicle.

Several lorries roared past – narrowly missing the dazed captain sahib – and he was indeed fortunate that the observant driver of the company water lorry noticed him and picked him up.

Before leaving Bergen I took Don Hughes down to Westwing's seaport office. Paul Paulsen, the chief pilot, was there and not happy with the weather forecast. Knowing how much depended on a clear day for the 13th, he had kept a close watch on reports for the Jostedal area and gave me the picture as he saw it.

'It has been fairly settled for four or five days now but too cloudy for your purposes. Tomorrow it may clear briefly but bad weather is coming from the west, from Scotland, and a lot of it. Rain and low cloud for several days is what you must expect once this low depression arrives from Britain. Of course one cannot tell: but to face reality, it looks bad for you.'

I thanked him and confirmed that we would telephone from Loen as soon on the 13th as conditions allowed – if indeed they did. Don disappeared into the little floating hangar to make an appraisal of the Cessna seaplane from which we would jump.

* * *

Two Norwegian public relations men from British Leyland showed us a quick route north from Bergen to Voss. They had cameras with telescopic attachments. Their car would dash on until it was several curving bends ahead of our convoy, then stop in the middle of the road, one of the men jumping out and snapping away furiously at the approaching expedition.

This became hilarious when the Land-Rovers ground to a halt on the steepest of bends, clutches smoking and drivers cursing. The Leyland man fluttered around as though recording a royal entourage. With the camera glued to his eye, he ran backwards and to either side, alternately squatting, standing and grimacing with artistic ecstacy. But he was wearing a snappily tailored suit and

D

looked crestfallen, poor man, when his photographic antics caused him to kneel by the side of the road in the deepest and muddiest of puddles.

They left us as dusk approached and we reached Dragsvik in time to catch the last ferry over Sognefjord to Vangsnes. The roads were narrow and severely rutted in places but it was too late for other traffic and we made good progress through the high misty passes which lead down to Nordfjord and our destination.

The lights of the Hotel Alexandra in Loen were reflected in the lake from afar and by four a.m. we were fast asleep somewhere within its luxurious portals – but not before polishing off a sumptuous tray of salmon and goat's cheese sandwiches which we found awaiting execution in the dining-room. Since the manager had agreed to give the team fifty per cent reduction on all costs whilst staying at the hotel, the food tasted all the better.

* * *

Dappled ruffles of light danced up and down the curtains and the stuffy stench of sleeping men flourished, for the central heating was full on and the windows shut. I stretched and kicked away the feather-bed cover, shuffling through to the bathroom to submerge my face in cold water. Sunlight streamed through the window, and my watch said nine o'clock as I pushed the window open and, standing on the lavatory seat, looked right out and above to the blue skies over the mountains. Above the highest glinting snow-capped peaks the odd pink halo hovered, mere furry suggestions of cloud, but everywhere else an almost mauve blue sky persisted which, somewhat deeper in hue, was repeated in the sparkling fjord. All the world was blue except the merry red roofs of Loen village and the glistening black bastions of rock which soar out of the lake half-way to the heavens.

What of the meteorological forecast? I glanced to the west but there too saw no blemish to the cerulean vista. I remembered how, four years ago, the weather here had deceitfully changed without warning but with alarming speed, catching a German expedition with its pants down, with fatal results. I washed, dressed and went downstairs to telephone Westwing. Mr. Paulsen was up and about and confirmed that Bergen too was basking under a cloudless sky.

'But,' he warned, 'the met. office have again confirmed that the bad spell is on its way. They estimate it will reach your area by midday preceded by high winds and low clouds.'

I asked him if he had a plane available that very morning should we put the jump forward a day. He said he would find out, so I agreed to ring again in an hour.

To advance the whole schedule twenty-four hours seemed on the face of it fairly simple, but in practice there were problems.

I.T.N. would not be pleased should their man miss the whole event, and there would anyway be little time to charter a helicopter for him, a machine which I.T.N. would pay for and had stressed was vital if good film was to be shot. The Land-Rovers would have to be completely unpacked and the equipment sorted out to prepare the glacier team's rucksacks and parachute bundles. The bundles themselves would have to be carefully fashioned and strapped. All this would take time. It was well past nine o'clock and, according to the forecast, the weather would hold for less than three hours – three hours in which Don and his pilot would have to be contacted, and their plane made ready. I had visions of Don sleeping off the previous night's festivities, for Bergen is a gay place. He would know the 12th was our day of reconnaissance at the Briksdalsbre and there was no reason why he should suspect that the jump might be put forward, for we had only discussed the possibilities of postponement.

The men were extremely tired after the crossing and the uncomfortable ten-hour drive. I knew that if they were left they would probably sleep on till midday.

To cancel the afternoon's reconnaissance of the Briksdalsbre glacier and river would be folly, for it was to be our escape route back to civilisation two weeks later and, although I had checked its face from below during the spring, I had only been able to see its last sheer ice-fall. I knew that it towered above this final cliff for a further two thousand feet of frozen ice, but no one had been able to advise me of its accessibility. The guide had made no comment when I told him of our intention to descend it but it was an unknown quantity and none of the team, I felt sure, would want to come down it without prior knowledge of its nature. Since none of them had ice-climbing experience it was only fair that they should see the size of the glacier in time to withdraw prudently should its very magnitude make them think twice. If we jumped that morning their first sight of the Briksdalsbre would be from its top-most ice-fall and then it might be too late to withdraw.

But surely all these drawbacks were flea-bites which must be accepted, since the only alternative – to wait twenty-four hours – might result in the total failure of the project. Once the low-pressure belt reached the Jostedal it could stay for weeks without a break. The very thought decided me.

Paul Paulsen had been waiting by his phone. As soon as I rang him he confirmed that the plane would be ready in an hour. Having divined my decision, he had already sent for Don and the pilot, so the Cessna should be at Loen before midday.

Initial prodding at the gently heaving shrouds in the bedrooms assigned to the expedition had little effect. Then I announced in a low tone that we would be jumping at noon: the sheets became animated, almost electrified, in the ensuing commotion as their bleary-eyed occupants surfaced with speed.

'Today,' groaned Geoff. 'I could have slept till pub-opening time.'

Once the time problem had sunk in, everyone was up with alacrity and, after a quick breakfast, out by the lakeside finding their parachutes, skis and a hundred small items which would make life liveable in the world of ice where they would be working for the next two weeks.

Soon the grass was littered with equipment and the word had spread amongst the four hundred tourists at the hotel. Stories of our origin and intentions were greatly exaggerated and muddled.

'So you're the guys who're trying to kill youselves up on the glayceers,' remarked a bald American with a necklace of camera accessories. 'I'd better get a photo of you boys while you're still all around.'

David Murray-Wells was having trouble with his rope. A hundred-foot coil of nylon with a breaking strain of two thousand pounds is quite bulky and difficult to stow on one's body when two parachutes are strapped to back and stomach as well. I suggested we put the ropes around our shoulders after the parachutes were in position but Geoff vetoed this.

'The coils would be blown all over the place in the slipstream,' he explained, 'and when you came to pull your handle it would be obstructed by rope. You would then panic and go into a spin or a dive. Better to secure the coils round your neck and strap the 'chutes over them.'

These ropes were carried by each parachutist together with a selection of rock and ice pitons, karabiner retaining rings and 'jumar' rope climbers. As the hour of reality approached, we each tried to visualise the course of action we might take should we miss the vital target of the ice plateau. Thermal winds, fierce down-draughts, sheer cliffs for thousands of feet and – at the edge of the ice – razor-edged fissures where the crevasse fields lie in wait like spiders' webs. A rope and pitons would be of little use to a parachutist dashed against the rock at forty miles an hour – faster in a down-draught. Nor would there be much time to climb the vertical walls of a ninety-foot crevasse before the blood froze and hands became useless.

We each had a miniature Sarbe radio with us. By flicking a lever on its control panel, a distress beacon is immediately activated on the international distress frequency. A rescue helicopter could home on to this beacon should anyone be blown away and lost.

By midday Geoff had prepared the parachute bundles, and a helicopter had been chartered for the I.T.N. photographer. The latter had arrived at Loen with Patrick Brook, both looking replete after their coastal journey, and John Collins was soon down on the jetty filming the preparations with his outsize Arriflex.

'A nice change to Belfast,' he declared, 'where they seem to think all cameramen are black protestants.'

A hotel steward arrived at the jetty with a silver salver, and on it a telegram from England. It was from my literary agent, George Greenfield, to wish us luck. He also mentioned that our contract with the *Telegraph* Colour Supplement had fallen through and he had now obtained the sponsorship of *The Sunday Times*. Our photographs and reports were to be sent back to that newspaper whenever possible.

A flickering sputnik to the west grew larger, dropping lower than the mountainous horizon and materialising in outline as it approached the jetty. The red and white fuselage was recognisable with a Westwing sign over the rear door.

Don was with us, and in a business-like mood. The pilot was

soon removing the Cessna's rear door and, glancing again to the west for the umpteenth time that morning, I knew the reason for their urgency. An unbroken screen of grey cloud rose slowly over the mountain range to the north-west of Innviksfjord.

Don was determined to drop all his human bundles on to their distant target before it was obscured by the fast-approaching cloudbank and scoured by treacherous wind currents. He had brought smoke canisters with him in metal brackets which he bade Roger strap to his ankles. Shortly after jumping, Roger would pull out the safety pins and a tell-tale streamer of smoke would help Don to observe his descent towards the ice.

Geoff put on a helmet with a cine-camera mounted to one side and a sighting lens positioned over his left eye. A cable ran down the sleeve of his orange anorak to end in a spring-mounted plunger. As he flew through the air with arms outspread, Geoff should be able to film Roger falling away below him simply by aiming his head and pressing the plunger with one thumb. This was the theory but Geoff was soon to regret having worn the Dalek-like helmet.

All of us wore light blue ski-ing suits beneath fluorescent orange anoraks. Small Union Jacks, a few the right way up, adorned each shoulder. Thick blue socks and British army boots completed the outlandish appearance of the team as Don ordered us down to the jetty to learn how to jump from the little seaplane without breaking our necks on its floats or rudders. If only we had been able to practise on a Cessna seaplane at Netheravon, our confidence would have been less shaky. It was not the same as the real thing, for we could not simulate the tremendous tug of the slipstream, nor jump away from the float – since the fjord water was unpleasantly cold. But we did find that chalk and cheese were about as similar as was the Cessna to the Rapides from which all our earlier practice had been effected.

Instead of simply grasping a wing-strut with both hands and planting both feet on the nearby bottom wing, one had to reach precariously from the little door to a narrow wing-bar which was neither vertical nor horizontal. Then a well-aimed lurch from the doorway to reach the float below with one's foot. Even with no slipstream and Don's helping hand this was not easy. Simply to let go of the wing strut in this position would be awkward and the body would almost certainly blow back into the float rudders. As Don carefully explained, we must jump sideways and outwards just before relaxing our grip of the strut. This would, he reckoned, avoid any injury to body or plane.

Once everyone had practised this unnatural manoeuvre and tried to memorise the feeling, Don lined us up on the jetty, checked each parachute minutely and exhorted us for a last time that one false move might be fatal. We were to remember all we had been told and, God willing, nothing would go wrong. He ordered the first group to climb into the little seaplane with him and signalled to the waiting pilot.

The crowds lining the jetty cheered and cameras whirred or clicked. Two other seaplanes left the lake with their crews of journalists and the helicopter was away with John Collins aboard.

My mouth felt dry and my stomach furry-lined as squadrons of butterflies free-fell within it. I would be first to jump and did not relish the idea. I glanced at the other parachutists. They looked unconcerned as the propeller vibrated into life and the steel floats surged out into the fjord.

Don was in the rear doorway shading his eyes, staring above the pinnacles to the south where long grey streamers of cloud, broken but persistent, hovered like ghostly vultures over the ice-fields of the Jostedal.

FOUR

The World's Toughest Jump

(*The Sunday Times*, August 14th, 1970)

THE CESSNA'S REAR DOORWAY was an upright oblong and from it we peered fascinated, almost mesmerised, at the successive vistas which flashed by as though the doorway were a cinema screen and we the cramped spectators. The fuselage was a small tube stripped of chairs and other accessories so that we sat on the smooth floor gripping one another's legs or the chair anchor-hooks to keep our heavily-laden bodies from sliding through the open doorway. Only Don stood, his back bent along the ceiling, trying no doubt to recall the route we had followed three years earlier to reach the black horn of the Lodalskåpa. Once this peak, the highest point of the Jostedalsbre, was sighted, the pilot would work out the relative position of our ice-field target and begin his climb into the thin air four thousand feet above the ice.

From time to time Don stooped to run a practised hand over our parachute packs, checking each nylon knot and metal toggle. It was a tight squeeze, so any quick movement against the fuselage might cause damage to our parachute fastenings and later result in a malfunction of the rip-cord.

The pilot knew these mountains well, and squeezed his Cessna between towering buttresses whence waterfalls poured in slow motion over glistening granite and steaming beds of dank lichen; blotting paper to the pulsating sheen of spray. Not more than fifty metres beneath us the rock had vanished: in its place a maze of serrated ice flanked the plateau. The lips of each crevasse were well delineated by a shimmering azure blue. These were the incredible fissures about which we had been warned: some were over a hundred feet in depth and would digest a parachutist complete with canopy, leaving no visible trace.

No one spoke as we watched – our hands were cold as sin; those of us without gloves shoving them between their legs for the warmth there. 'However cold it is,' I mused, 'it doesn't warrant the danger of gloves. How can I possibly feel the thin red handle, when I want it, with thick woollen gloves muting the perception of my questing fingers.'

An aromatic, almost sensual odour of body sweat tinged the cold metal smell of our temporary cabin. 'They are all sweating,' I thought with quick satisfaction, 'their adrenalin is pumping away ten to the dozen and they feel like vomiting just as I do.' I smiled at Don: he grinned down at me, sensing perhaps the confidence he exuded. I glanced at Peter. His mouth smiled but his eyes remained distant and his knuckles were white where he gripped the pilot's seat. Perhaps we were all thinking of the cliffs and the fissures, noticing how small was the white patch of the ice-field and knowing that it would be smaller yet when viewed from over ten thousand feet. There would be little margin for error.

* * *

A demoniac crackle and whine came from the pilot's headphones. He jammed them back over his close-cropped hair and twiddled a knob to his right. Glancing over his shoulder at Don, he shrugged and shook his head.

He had been speaking to the pilot of another Cessna, carrying photographers . . . they had located the chosen ice-field but it was not as wide as had been thought, since the previous winter had not brought much snow. Crevasse fields away from the edge of the plateau are usually well covered with snow, but this year many fissures had remained uncovered by snow bridges, so smooth areas were few and far between.

Our pilot finally raised a gloved hand: he too had located our dropping zone and now circled above it to give Don a chance to appraise its limitations. Don showed the pilot two fingers – denoting the height of ascent he required. The Cessna shuddered with increased throttle and the floor lurched as we climbed.

Levelling out at two thousand feet over the Lodalskåpa, the pilot set a circular course which traversed the landing area on its upwind run.

Don was now crouching rigid in the doorway, mottled skin sucked taut against his skull and lips drawn back in a fixed snarl as the slipstream tugged at his head. His dark glasses would have been whipped off and away but were well stuck to his cheeks with black adhesive tape . . . There are no flies on Don – parachuting is a game where little omissions may lead to disaster.

His hand jerked out into the slipstream, deftly releasing a furled streamer: it jinked away, its orange fabric tail unrolling as it fell. Its flight path told us nothing but, to Don, it acted as an anemometer, telling him the speed and direction of the various wind currents between us and the ice. He must remember the exact position of its release relative to its landing spot and form a mental picture of the landscape below, knowing thereby precisely when and where to release his human loads to give them a fair chance of landing on smooth ice: a deadly game of darts only for an expert.

Although the drop would take place from this noted position along the oval of the Cessna's course, we must first climb another two thousand to ten thousand feet. This would give us an ample safety margin, after leaving the aircraft, in which to achieve a stable falling position. Whilst falling we would count out the seconds and pull our rip-cords at the height at which the streamer had left the Cessna. Thereafter we were in the grip of the same wind currents – unless of course they had changed during the short interim period.

By steering the parachutes correctly, we could add five miles an hour to the speed at which we might travel in any down-wind direction or, conversely, subtract five miles an hour by steering up-wind, for the 'chutes are designed to travel at five miles an hour in nil wind conditions. So, however strong the wind, we would not be entirely at its mercy unless forced to pull the rip-cord too high.

This must have been worrying Peter in particular for he had every reason to believe that he would become badly unstable. In over twenty jumps at Netheravon he had performed a number of dangerous manoeuvres whilst desperately attempting to get the knack of stability. He had always been able to pull the rip-cord before his aerobatics became too dangerous, and since there are empty fields for many miles around Netheravon, his only penalty was a long walk back to the hangars.

But this was not Netheravon and Peter knew it. Of all the team, he had the most reason for fear. I admired his quiet courage immensely and prayed that all would go well for him. I felt glad I was not in his boots and relatively confident that I would be able to gain and maintain a stable position for the full fourteen seconds.

It had been so sunny and clear that day three years ago with little or no wind. We had had the large Otter plane then and had jumped from much lower. Now grey wreaths moved below us in growing density hiding the ice-face completely from time to time: not a serious hazard yet, but Don must be thinking of the next three flights to follow when conditions would be worse.

The engine sound had eased slightly: we had stopped climbing and in a minute would be circling into the final up-wind run over the dropping zone.

Don moved back from the door suddenly and beckoned us urgently to get ready.

Awkwardly, and careful not to brush the 'chutes against one another, we levered ourselves into kneeling positions facing the maw.

This was the moment of truth from which there could be 'no honourable withdrawal,' as the military books put it. I knew not to look down or, indeed, out into space. To the very last minute I must look at my watch-strap, the fuselage or even a stud on the doorway – for my single ungovernable fear was not so much the act of jumping itself; it was the fearful thought that one glimpse of the ice, of the black peaks below, would bring alive all the latent terrors of the dream world: the nightmarish feeling of cartwheeling away into nothingness, mouth frozen open in a silent retching scream. To let one niggling thought of that nature through the gate of the mind would be fatal – for a flood of irrepressible apprehension might follow, and who really trusts the strength of his own will?

Not I, so I concentrated fiercely on the solid objects within the fuselage and mentally rehearsed the robot-like actions which make up the perfect exit, remembering the raucous commands of the Netheravon instructors.

'Head well back as you jump . . . look at the doorway.' (This was a pipe-dream in my case for I invariably screwed my eyes tight shut for the seconds of leaving the aircraft.)

'Shove that stomach forward . . . spread all your limbs like you was jumping for joy!'

And Don's last warning – specific to the Cessna. 'She's not a Rapide, so don't treat her like one. You must jump outwards away from the plane not just backwards in the normal fashion.'

I imagined my reaction should the 'chute not deploy when I pulled its rip-cord. Exactly where would I find that little reserve handle which I normally forgot about?

Then I felt a rough hand shake my shoulder. Don was shouting at me with urgency and pointing out meaningfully.

But something was wrong. I had been subconsciously awaiting the dreaded sound of the engines cutting back; the necessary preliminary to any free-fall jump which slows the plane down to just above its stalling speed, minimising the power of the slipstream past the fuselage. The Cessna was still at maximum speed. I pointed at the pilot desperately but Don gestured, very firmly, out of the door. There was no arguing and I forced an arm through the bucketing slipstream to grip the wing-strut, then with some effort the other arm. This was ridiculous – I would never get into a reasonable, safe position on the float with this roaring sucking force tearing me away.

I shall never quite know what happened next. Three years ago at the vital moment, one of the team had lost his nerve and Don had helped him on his way with a friendly and well-timed push. I was fearful lest he should think I too was hesitating and give me an ignominious shove. Perhaps for this reason I was too hurried, for, gripping the wing-strut – as a drowning man clutches a branch – I lurched my legs towards the float below. Rubber boots scrabbling on the wet metal for a hold and hands – numb with the biting cold – gradually losing their grip on the strut, the wind force took full hold of my body. Much in the manner of an unseen squid sucking a shellfish from rock, the slipstream tore me loose and flung me away, a puppet with no strings. Unable therefore to jump outwards, my body passed close by the fuselage and a sharp pain in my hand as it struck the float side registered briefly.

'One thousand and one, one thousand and two . . .' Netheravon training had sunk in, for my disembodied voice was chiming out the seconds automatically and I opened my eyes. 'It's so very cold – I will freeze solid in this ridiculous position,' I remember thinking. Then there was that insidious feeling that my body was going into a spin. Fearfully I stretched my arms wider and pushed forward my stomach. 'One thousand and five, one thousand and six . . .' But the spin was becoming more pronounced. I glanced down at my legs and knew why; the left one was kicking desperately, convulsively, like a dying rabbit. I suppose it was instinctively trying to kick me back into a stable position but was in fact having an adverse effect. It had seemingly acquired a mind of its own and only with a great effort of will could I control it and force the whole leg outwards. 'One thousand and nine . . .'

The world was suddenly a peaceful, silent, faraway place above which my body floated, chanting its numerical litany, with absolutely no sense of movement or urgency. But only for fleeting seconds, for I was now flying at close on a hundred and thirty miles an hour and every limb must be perfectly positioned to remain stable at this speed.

They weren't however, for my head must still have been slightly inclined after watching the antics of my leg. Slowly, almost imperceptibly, its angle had caused the inverted saucer-shape of the falling body to tilt forwards. 'One thousand and twelve . . .' I was going into a dive and the sudden realisation caused panic. Both arms snapped inwards to the rip-cord, searching for the cold feel of it – but a ciné-camera was loose inside my anorak having slipped down and was pressed by the wind over the handle bar. Now my position was bunched and haywire. Grovelling in the folds of the anorak, as for gold dust, I found the red handle and ripped it away viciously, arms returning to the star position to halt a rapidly materialising somersault.

Perhaps two seconds later the crack, as of a whip, and the breath-taking arrest of the securing harness had me dangling happily beneath a full orange canopy. The harness straps were twisted high up but by the laws of elasticity soon unwound themselves and through them, to the north, I saw another canopy floating towards and well above me; the parachutist too small to recognise. I tried to reach into the anorak's neck to retrieve my ciné-camera but the chest harness was too tight to allow its egress and I felt again a throbbing pain from one hand: looking at it, I found it purple and swollen like a half tennis-ball. A pity, for I would miss the chance of taking some good film but the helicopter must be up there somewhere with John Collins making hay for I.T.N. while the sun shone, although the machine had been conspicuously absent during our climb up above the ice.

Looking down between my legs, there were streamers of mist blowing before the wind and below them thousands of feet of dark void – most uninviting; but to the left the jagged white edge of the table top not more than a thousand feet below. My boots seemed to be moving fast along a parallel course to the glacier's flank, which was not reassuring since I must be descending at a good twenty miles an hour. After a hard tug on the left-hand toggle, the canopy turned and tacked across the wind making slow but sure progress to the south.

Now the great angled fissures of the ice-fringe passed beneath my limp legs – God forbid landing amongst that lot – then the crevasses grew narrower, more like thin blue veins. Directly ahead a lone black outcrop of curious fragmentation: surely, that was the Braeniba. Then it was past to the left and the wind was sighing as I swung like a pendulum. Everything now was close and white. The ice must be rushing up to meet me but there was no perspective, no way of telling how far away was the white mass nor precisely when I would crash into it. I braced my legs, knees bent, for the impact . . . 'head and elbows tucked in and boots below bottom'.

A fleeting glimpse of orange to the right – someone else was already down – and the slightly suffocating jolt of a beautifully soft landing – not on ice but packed snow. Wiping some from my mouth and nose, I got up to look around but was dragged over again as a strong surface wind caught the billowing canopy and pulled it along like an ice-yacht. By pulling in several lengths of a single 'chute cord, I collapsed the material and ran round to the leeward side before removing the harness.

A series of fluctuating and bitterly cold gusts came across the ice-field and I wished there was a sweater or two under my anorak instead of the cotton ski-shirt.

The others were carefully restacking their 'chutes within their retaining packs; an irritating task for it was important to keep all moisture from the canopy panels before folding them. The nylon would otherwise rot with damp in time – and all our expensive 'chutes would eventually have to return to Netheravon for use by many other aspiring free-fallers.

We were shivering slightly by the time a faint rhythmic drone announced the Cessna's return, for there was no cover or sheltering nook on the sloping ice-field. Once the plane was visible to the north-west, Patrick lit two flares. It had said 'BLUE' on the army tins but they were burning away an unashamed white, slightly fluorescent, which might well go unnoticed by the plane. But the pilot evidently had a definite bearing on the dropping zone this time and soon saw us, waggling his wings before climbing to 10,500 feet for the second drop. My anorak was rippling, smacking loose folds against its canvas belt, for the wind was more persistent now. 'Eighteen knots,' I thought, 'possibly stronger from time to time.' Then for a period it would drop away almost entirely – very awkward weather for a parachutist and stronger than during the first drop. The clouds too were scudding by, hiding the Cessna now and then as it climbed; but they seemed more like pockets of mist than the substantial rainclouds we were expecting.

The others who had been on the first flight had experienced the same difficulties with the slipstream as myself but fortunately without injury. I wondered how the second group would fare. They were the better, more experienced, parachutists, but conditions were now anything but safe.

Bob Powell's diary records the afternoon in succinct terms:

1600 hours: The first group emplane. The aircraft is away an hour when we hear the voice of the pilot come over the radio from a seaplane parked by the Alexandra's jetty saying 'All dropped – mission successful'.

We struggle into our kit, struggle being the operative word since, in addition to parachutes and reserves, we are carrying ropes, cameras, and smoke grenades. The dropping height for our lift is to be 10,300 or 10,500 feet if the pilot can make it.

The cloud has closed in a good deal while we await the return of the aircraft.

Shortly after take-off and quite without warning the other (closed) rear door flew open and Geoff found himself looking out of the door somewhat prematurely.

. . . the cross-pull which I am doing for only the third time works excellently and the pack deploys without any problem. The most perfect jump I have ever experienced but two of the others were carried very close to the crevasses.

There is a tremendous feeling of elation as 'chutes are packed and we await the heavy drop coming in.

Roger Chapman is a master of understatement but his diary is more explicit:

. . . as we boarded the Cessna, we could see the storm clouds scurrying across the sky heralding the dark thunder in the west, and we could feel the wind begin to stiffen – it was going to be a race against time to get to the glacier before the storm. We sensed the look of urgency in Don Hughes's face. Ten minutes later we flew over the edge of the glacier but still climbed. Don pointed his finger through the open doorway. Down below we could see small black dots on the white surface of the glacier marking the target area; also marked by two smoke flares. There was one minute to go. Very quickly my mind went through the drill. 'Remember to pull the grenade first, then count.'

The pilot could not, or did not, know that he had to cut the engines and as a result the noise of wind and the force of the slipstream was fantastic. Bob sat in the exit, pushed off and was whipped away from sight in a flash. The wind has sprung up quite hard now. The others are turning towards the dropping zone and driving as hard as they can. Suddenly, I realise why.

Brendan with a frozen lemming.

Some of Brendan – the biologist's – specimens after his descent from the icecap. He found a Collembola hitherto unknown in Norway.

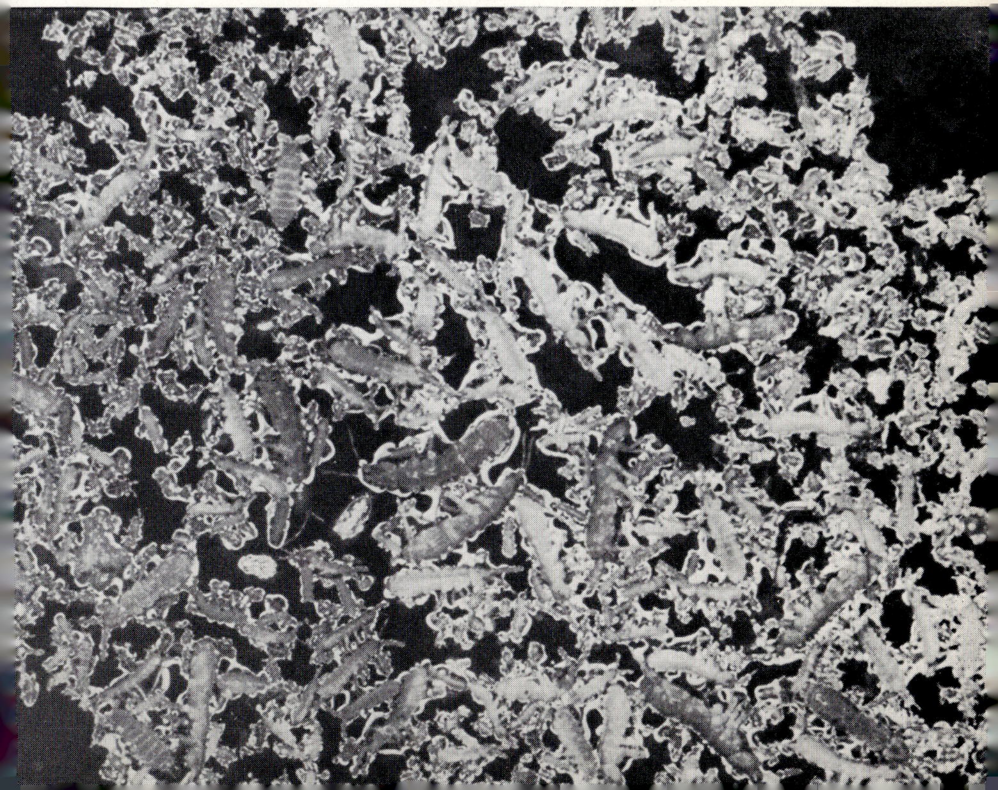

At dawn above the Briksdalsbre. The flag had become smaller during the night

The mists clear above the Briksdalsbre and we break camp. *Left to right:* Roger Chapman, Ranulph Fiennes, Patrick Brooke, Bob Powell, Geoff Holder.

There is a large drop over the side of the glacier beneath us to the left . . . In fact we land rather too close to the edge of the glacier. . .

Owing to the curving nature of the ice-field it appeared extremely alarming when the last two parachutists of the second group disappeared from view into dead ground; for we knew the cliffs fell away precisely where they had vanished. Both Geoff and Roger, for it was they, had landed close to one another beyond our ice-field and no more than a hundred yards from 'outer space' as Peter described it.

When Geoff arrived at our marshalling point by the flare, the bridge of his nose was lacerated, both eyelids swollen and discoloured, and he looked in some pain as he walked. It transpired that the Cessna's violent slipstream had knocked him away sideways causing the metal sighting visor of his camera helmet to press violently downwards on his face. His ribs too had suffered bruising against the float and were hurting him as he breathed. But how lucky he had retained consciousness.

Geoff's diary records his landing:

. . . having spent some time filming I had ended up in a somewhat awkward spot, however, with my Para Commando 'chute, I was able to land on the dropping zone general area, though only seventy-five yards from the precipice. Having not been worried until now, I suddenly was – I found I was being dragged to within twenty-five yards of the ice-edge, my ribs causing some pain . . .

The team was now complete and fanned out into a wide circle around the dropping zone leaving only Patrick and Henrik with the flare tins. The wind moaned over the ice-fields and it crossed my mind how easily our equipment might be prevented from reaching us. Then we would be in a pretty pickle. No tents, sleeping-bags or spare clothes, nothing between us and the biting cold of the ice at six thousand feet. Don would know our plight and do his best to drop the bundles in our area, but it was more than likely some would go over the edge. I had a fleeting image of some astonished Scandinavian farmer in a distant valley praising God with particular sincerity next Sunday and supplementing his family dinner with expedition goodies. Bob and two others spread out along the edge of the ice-field but clear of the crevasses in the hope of reaching and collapsing any canopies that might come down near the brink, before they were blown over and away.

To heave heavy bundles accurately from the shifting platform of a small plane is extremely tricky even without the fear of damaging its rear fuselage, even without fragile floats and rudders below the doorway, for it is necessary to balance each bundle right at the exit point shortly before heaving it out. At this stage, there is a battle between the crew and the slipstream, the latter trying to tear the bundle and its canopy away prematurely.

Only once had I tried my hand at the precise art of 'the cargo dropmaster' (a skill which is apparently simple once perfected). High over the Qara' Jebel mountains in Dhofar, circling above an isolated camp of the Sultan of Muscat's forces, and hopefully out of range of rebel gunfire, I had volunteered to help Captain Mike Kelly drop mail and rations from his Beaver. Much was my horror, and great his scorn and cursing, when the first bundle – slightly too far out into the doorway perhaps – was caught by the wind and, try as I would, I could not prevent it from whipping away into the slipstream.

Long afterwards I felt guilty on seeing anyone from that particular camp, for word had got around as to the identity of the culprit, and no one had liked to see their mail floating tantalisingly into rebel hands.

Still thinking of Dhofar, I stood waiting for our gear to drop, when who should appear but Captain Guy Sheridan. With him was a young Norwegian girl – Norway's junior langlauf champion. The two of them were out training for the next Winter Olympics. They had appeared quite suddenly out of the mist, leaving Roger Chapman as startled as an astronaut would be at meeting human beings on Mars. Roger greeted them with a few words of salutary Norwegian, and was much surprised at Guy's: 'Hello, how's it going?'

Guy had been most helpful to us in obtaining equipment from the Royal Marines before we came out, so he knew why we were on the glacier. He and his Norwegian friend were on their way to their camp which lay to the east. Guy said that there was a flat route over the glacier to the Fåberg ice-arm which he knew and we should follow his ski tracks from the dropping zone in order to gain the upper reaches of the Fåbergstølsbre. A mist was creeping over the ice-fields so they left us; gliding silently over the white slopes with that long graceful lope achieved only after many months of practice and expert tuition.

We had been in the Oman together for many months and I remembered that Guy had caught the ski-racing 'bug' just before being posted to the Middle East. However, undeterred by his posting, he had continued to train for the Army Ski team. I had gone off to the ancient Arab town of Rostaq to see him one week-end only to be informed by his Arab orderly that he was away on the Jebel, 'Every day he run like a horse many miles up the mountain. Maybe he is mad. He carries long sticks in both hands and goes faster than a Land-Rover.' Since it was well over 100 degrees in the shade most days of the Omani summer, this seemed unlikely and I was amazed when Guy appeared shortly afterwards, in the mess garden, bathed in sweat and carrying a ski-stick in either hand. Throughout the summer he ran a daily six miles during the murderous afternoons when all Arabs and most 'sahibs' lie down and do nothing.

Then we moved south to rebellious Dhofar where no one moved outside the camp without an armed escort. But Guy kept on running along the sandy beach and a Land-Rover with an orderly cruised alongside in case of snipers. Guy left several months before the rest of us, having been selected for the British Army Cross Country Ski team so his persistence had been rewarded. Shortly after he departed, a band of guerrillas visited the same stretch of beach that he had trained on and killed one of the Sultan's chief intelligence men in his house beneath the palms . . .

A shout brought me back to immediate reality.

'Something's come loose,' Peter was pointing at one of the pink canopies floating high above us. The kit-drop was under way and, sure enough, a dark object had parted company with one bundle and was falling towards us. It smashed into the packed snow not a hundred yards away; one of the larger radios. Initial inspection disclosed no apparent damage, but it had landed at close on eighty miles an hour and its innards must have suffered a severe jolt.

Later we fitted batteries to it and were not surprised that the set was dead as a doornail.

We were certainly too far south for any light effects of the Aurora Borealis but, as twilight drew nigh, the view from our perch on the sloping plateau was striking and not easily forgotten. It must have been well past eight o'clock and the setting sun played games of visual fantasy with our world of ice. A vast and gentle swathe of violet shot with orange ruffles outlined the eastern horizon and over all the shimmering fields of prehistoric ice lay the moon shadow of the Lodalskåpa. Its ugly, almost phallic horn rose gloomy from a host of lesser peaks, glimmering faintly in outline through the haze of dusk.

A humming drone with no directional source came to us with the moaning winds, but it was the blinking red glow of its tail-light which first heralded the Cessna flying low over the plateau as it approached for the fourth and last drop. Patrick lit a flare – this one was blue – and the plane came in very low over us before veering away to climb. It must have been almost too dark to see within the unlit fuselage as Brendan and Don prepared the remaining bundles.

Brendan later told us of the anxious moments he had spent trying to haul Don bodily back into the fuselage; for they had resorted to a unique method of despatch.

After landing at Loen a second time Don had decided that they must alter the plans for the equipment drop. Accordingly they had thrown out the bundles with Don strapped to a float by a safety line. As the bundles were passed into the doorway by Brendan, Don would grasp them momentarily, but sufficiently to ensure their avoiding the floats and the delicate rudder cables.

Once this task was completed he had tried to climb back to the doorway, but the slipstream had held him tenaciously and it had taken Brendan many minutes to haul Don through the door.

The last 'chute away, the Cessna dived low and 'buzzed' us, wings waggling, before turning north over the valleys of Nordfjord to be lost in the spiralling gullies of Bödal.

We would have to spend the night in the shelter of the Braeniba rocks close by, so all hands were set to the loading of sledges with the heavier items – the rubber boats and 600-foot rope coils – and the tents were pitched amongst the haphazard mass of centralised items under a sheer granite cliff. Blocks of snow were shovelled into makeshift walls round each tent and tiny metal cookers were soon blazing away beneath tins of dehydrated curry or beef broth. Climbing through the entrance hole of the mini-tent I shared with Patrick, I was shocked to see – by the light of a flickering candle – that he had been wearing a pair of woman's full-length pantees under his ski-trousers. This was a revelation: poking my head out of the tent again to find some willing ears to hear this damning news, I saw to my horror that Roger – standing some distance from his tent to answer nature's call – was clad in similar black pantees.

'Aren't you cold?' I asked him.

'Not at all, they're fantastically warm. Bob Powell's wife gave some of us a pair before we left Newcastle.'

I imagined a cutting in *The Sunday Times* that week: 'The see-through craze reaches new bounds as a team of British scientists in woman's underwear parachute on to Europe's largest glacier.'

FIVE

Bright Skies Deceive

THURSDAY, AUGUST 13TH. Away to the west a golden eagle soared high above the silken snake of the Nigardsbre. Faint orange pigmentation appeared spread like a thin layer of butter over the grey ice-crust, for the sun touches the frozen slopes of Jostedal long before the distant fjord villagers or their cockerels sense the dawn.

Patrick stirred and sighed: he had tossed back and forth during the night rather like the princess with the pea under her mattress, only our mattress was a bundle of unfurled equipment parachutes and one of the metal harness clips had plagued him throughout the night, biting into his hip.

Condensation droplets had formed on the low tent ceiling and, waking, we contemplated a fine furry hoar frost on its inner nylon lining. The army boots we had jumped in were hard as wood, but our langlauf boots and socks had spent the night in our sleeping-bags with us and so were dry and malleable. We lit a gas-cooker and brewed tea between us. Patrick looked unkempt and I told him so.

'You look about ninety yourself,' he said with indignation, 'and there's milk powder all over your chin. The sooner the sun comes out the better, this place is like a morgue.'

The tea was good and moaning grunts from next door indicated a general stirring in the other tents. I poked my head from the entrance-hole into a chilling breeze: two of the tents were hidden from view, for their inmates, unlike the foolish frozen virgins we were, had cut square slabs of ice into surrounding walls to defeat the wind.

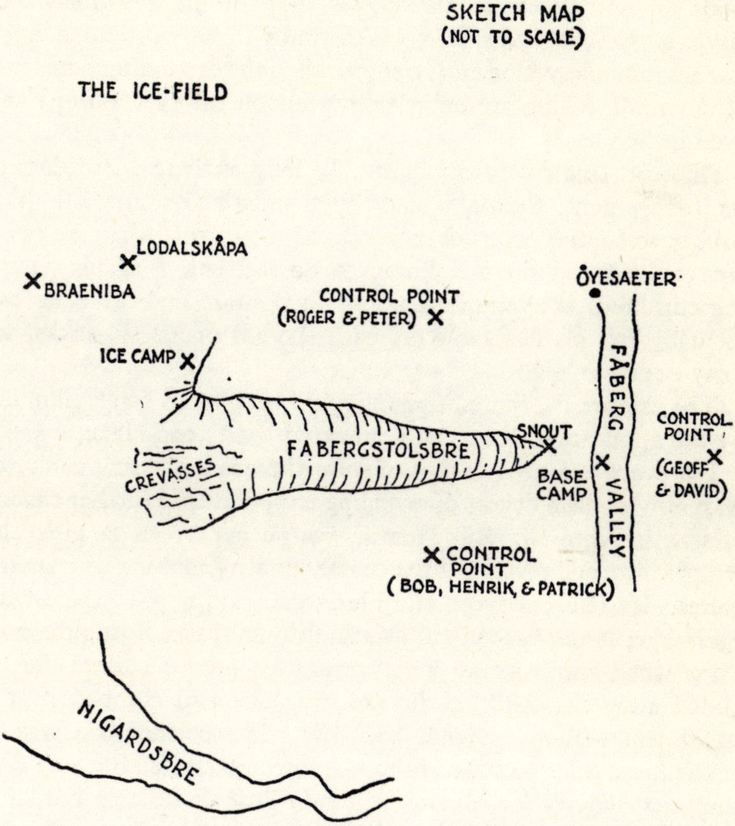

Soon we were up, the tents down, and the team divided into two groups of four to man the sledges. Since these were over six feet in length and a metre wide, they could take heavy loads if carefully stacked with well-balanced cargo. Our Avon rubber boat weighed a hundred pounds, and the 600-foot coils of Marlow rope were almost as heavy. After restacking the more bulky kit, and doling out items to each man to add to their rucksacks, we were still unable to find room for a theodolite, the radio and two of the tents. We left these by the Braeniba and clipped on the individually fitted langlauf skis which Henrik had waxed for us.

Langlaufing is a Scandinavian sport practised by very few Britons. Pioneers have tried to enthuse the British with its simplicity and economy but the countryside and weather conditions do not favour langlaufing as they do in Scandinavia or Bavaria. Nor, it seems, do we take kindly to a sport demanding a fair amount of exertion and strength when the expanding potentials of downhill ski-ing are effortlessly available all over Europe and even in Scotland.

One can langlauf in any clothes so long as there is freedom of limb movement. Specially made boots must be bought with thick rubber soles that protrude beyond the toe-caps so that the overlaps can be fitted into metal brackets on each ski. A spring retaining clip holds the toe of each boot in position and the skier can virtually run on flat snow or, with the aid of his ski-sticks, up forty-degree inclines.

The skis are prevented from slipping backwards when climbing by the application of specially prepared waxes and klisters.

For every conceivable type of snow there is a different colour of wax, and for each degree of changing temperature a further change of wax is required. But Henrik was an expert at gauging the temperature and texture of the coarse snow by rubbing some in his palms. He selected green and blue waxes and applied them with aggression to the base of our skis; finishing by massaging the now shiny wood with a cork. The preparation proved correct, for he glided away smoothly to the nearest slope and climbed it at a smart run with no evident back-slip. If too smooth a wax is applied, the skier will slide fast on a downhill stretch but will find climbing difficult for his skis will gain little or no grip but slide away backwards giving a treadmill effect to his efforts. On the other hand, an over-glutinous wax such as a klister resin, which is for wet or slushy snow, might be ideal for climbing but will cause clogging – with heavy layers of mushy snow sticking to each ski – allowing no free slide at all. When the correct wax is applied, fast movement up and downhill is possible, and once the rhythmic glide of the professional is learnt, distances of over fifty miles in a day can be attained without undue exertion.

In 1967 I had moved from the Braeniba rocks to the Fåbergstølsbre with a friend. On that occasion we had intended to descend the gentle Lodalsbre but had become lost in the maze of ice-fields. Remembering the occasion, I had asked Guy Sheridan the night before to leave ski-tracks from our camp to the top of the Fåbergstølsbre. Our intended ice camp – where the equipment, rations and radio base were to be established as a nerve centre for the survey work – was to be above and to one flank of the Fåberg ice-tongue. With the heavy sledges it was important to keep to high ground until the last moment, only to descend to the slopes of the Fåbergstølsbre when we arrived directly above the intended ice camp. To descend in error to either side of our goal would entail a dangerous traverse over the upper slopes of the ice-tongue since the glacier table is surrounded on every flank by deeply lacerated ice-fields. As soon as the ice begins its downward tumble over the edge of the table-top, it becomes fissured and dangerous, rumbling and creaking in response to gravity and the changing temperature.

We took map bearings on the southern flank of the Fåbergstølsbre and set off in the spoor marks of Guy Sheridan's skis. Their direction at first coincided with our compass bearing, lying south-east over the rolling plateau which slopes away from the Lodalskåpa feature.

The metal sledge-runners ripped hissing over the firm crust, each *půlk* harness strapped around the shoulders and waist of its human 'husky'. Two men skied behind each load with one of their ski-sticks pushing it to aid the lead-man whilst Henrik went ahead to locate and follow the barely visible spoor-line. The sun had risen above the distant Galdhŏppigen range and, perspiring with the exertion, we were soon stopping to remove sweaters and anoraks though it was good to be warm again after the biting cold of the Braeniba camp.

The hours passed and the front sledge, with Geoff straining at its harness, halted. Roger, sweating freely, turned round with a frown.

'By my reckoning we should have hit the Fåbergstølsbre half an hour ago. We must have come too far and I'm sure the tracks we're following have veered well south of our bearing.'

He was right: I had noticed the variation but hoped Guy was

simply detouring to avoid bad ground. Perhaps it would have been better to follow a bearing of our own from the Braeniba and ignore the ski-trail altogether. It was easy to say this in retrospect but at the time it had seemed wiser to follow the tracks of someone who knew the area rather than to blunder over unknown ice along a compass 'bee-line' which might well take us through hilly country, crevassed zones and rock outcrops.

A heated discussion ensued whilst the sledge 'huskies' were changed, and a compromise was reached with a new bearing to be followed to the east. Soon the ice-slopes fell away to our front and the sledges picked up speed, propelling their anxious 'huskies' before them as the incline became severe. Spotting the danger Henrik shouted back and, with Bob stemming his skis strongly behind the lead-sledge, they managed to halt its rapidly increasing rate of descent before the heavy *půlk* got out of control and turned over. Had it done so, it might well have dragged the harnessed Roger beneath its sharp metal runners. Henrik had seen this happen in Finland and, on his advice, we altered our tactics. The lead-men unstrapped their harnesses, and retaining straps were fixed to the sledge-chassis. By tacking diagonally down the long slopes, the pace decreased and we avoided accidents. Below and on the edge of the glacier's horizon the sinister lips of the first crevasses gleamed blue. A small black cluster of rock punctured the ice not unlike that which we knew to lie at the crest of the Fåbergstølsbre.

Roger took two back-bearings and concluded that we had indeed arrived above the correct glacial arm, for all the surrounding features related correctly to its position. But the rocks looked strange, for there was that about them which I could not place, though I wracked my memory for a mental picture of the sheltering rock-arm we had passed three years before which had pointed the way to the Fåbergstølsbre.

There was a general feeling of relief for everyone had feared the possibility of a crevasse-field between us and the ice-camp location. Only Henrik had much experience of ice or crevasse navigation, and what we had seen from the air the previous day had been daunting.

Patrick and I went ahead to the rock cluster – cautiously, for the whine and almost metallic groan of the crevasse-field was audible close by. Without moving out on to the fissured slope it was not possible to see the ice-tongue below, but I was still uncertain that this was the Fåbergstølsbre. The others had been convinced by the evidence of Roger's back-bearings, and, keen to waste no further time, were irritated at my havering. Still, better safe than sorry. Bearing in mind the old army adage that time spent in reconnaissance is seldom time wasted, I reflected how foolish we would look pitching camp above the wrong glacial arm and surveying the wrong *bre*!

Patrick, I felt sure, would agree with me. I remembered how, when he was acting as personal aide to the British Governor-General in Tasmania, he had led a convoy of staff cars full of top brass to inspect a large regimental camp in the 'out-back'.

Patrick had been to a number of parties just beforehand and had had no time to reconnoitre the whereabouts of the camp. Great was his surprise and subsequent disgrace when the convoy arrived after a long and dusty drive, at an abandoned, indeed derelict, army camp with the same name as the one awaiting inspection.

I followed Patrick along the edge of the broken ice. He was a strong skier with a long easy stride. Half an hour's climb to the north-east found us on a sharp promontory where, quite suddenly, a wide view to the north-east lay below us. The scenery was now familiar, jolting my memory so that I was back again three years earlier with Simon Gault sliding down the narrow ice-gully above Fåberg to stand in wonder as we watched the incredible majesty of our first glacier, the tumbling blue ice which runs like a frozen river for two thousand giddy feet into the black gloomy valley of Fåberg and Ǒysaeter.

Now I realised where we were and saw that we must have detoured well to the south of the Fåberg arm by following Guy's tracks and had arrived above the notorious Nigardsbre, a glacier which earlier this century advanced into the valley below, crushing farms that stood in its wake.

But we were below the level of the smooth ice, well below it, and on the southern flank of the Fåberg ice-arm. To reach the rock-cluster at the crest of its northern flank we must either face the back-breaking task of hauling the heavy sledges back up to the smooth ice of the plateau and ski north until directly above the rock-cluster, or else traverse over the upper regions of the ice-tongue itself which would involve little climbing and should be a far quicker route. The only danger involved with the latter course was the lack of snow lying over the ice-tongue. Three years before it had been a vast white slope with thickly packed snow covering the fissures. I borrowed Patrick's binoculars and scanned the field from our vantage point to the distant shelter of the rock outcrop. There were long snaking seams of dirty snow but the overall effect was grey streaked by darkly shadowed furrows. Whether or not these fissures still had sufficient snow-cover to bridge them, we could only discover by attempting the crossing.

Patrick surveyed the icy vista with confidence.

'We're only in mid-August and although the snow is melting fast you can plainly see the snow-bridges are intact over parts of most of the fissures. Even if the snow is fairly rotten it should hold our weight if we keep moving briskly. I'm all for trying it. Anything to avoid pulling those bloody sledges up to the plateau.'

Looking up I saw what he meant. We would never reach the table-top again in this heat before dusk. Strange that one should be sweating freely at the least exertion in this world of ice. It only needed a cloud over the sun or a breeze to set one shivering but now we had our shirts off and socks rolled down.

I remembered a strange journey Patrick and I had once made in the 'forbidden mountains' of the Oman. As usual Patrick had been unfit and grumbled continuously as we climbed from sea level to the 10,000 feet peaks, stumbling up vertiginous mule-tracks where narrow steps had been cut into sheer rock by the ancient Persian invaders. Patrick had refused to bring a rifle although this was the Jabal al Akhdar; recent stronghold of the Imam's rebels where no Europeans travel without an armed escort. I had a small bolt-action rifle and Patrick condescended to carry five rounds for it. The temperature was over 110 degrees Fahrenheit and we kept our rucksacks light, though Patrick, a lover of small comforts, had contrived to bring tinned fish sent him by Fortnum and Masons and a full bottle of Glenfiddich whisky. Our water-bottles were empty and we were making for a little mountain spring known as Salut. I had been there once a year before with an Army patrol, but somehow lost the way.

Patrick's cynical remarks about my navigation grew more and more dry as his throat became parched but, as I impressed on him, it was only through his own tortoise-like pace that we failed to reach Salut that night. Instead an inky blackness covered us whilst still groping along narrow paths with an appalling drop below. We decided to stop for the night and quench our thirst with Glenfiddich. Thoughts of the oft rebellious Benni Hinna tribesmen who inhabit the mountains prompted us to climb above the track and we found a smooth ledge at the top of our precipice. After a delicious snack of unseen fish and whisky, Patrick made a final bedtime remark about my evil memory and then threw the empty fish tin at the invisible ledge behind us: there was no sound. I could hear Patrick sit bolt upright in the darkness and we listened together intensely – then from far below came a faint echoing tinkle. Our ledge was not the main mountain-top after all but the knife-edge of a peak with as great a drop to our rear as that which we had just climbed up to our front. We spent the night huddled together, indecently close, and great was our relief at first light on the morrow to climb back to the mule-track and terra firma.

Patrick had always struck me as an excellent type for an expedition but great was my surprise when he volunteered to join us on the Jostedal, for his motto was 'any fool can be uncomfortable'. He was a man who would do anything to avoid discomfort or exertion, bad food or soiled linen and yet when such evils were inescapable, he would survive the most harrowing experience with humour and cynicism. He appeared incapable and ineffective – almost a dilettante – but was in reality highly dependable.

I followed him back to the sledge teams, gliding fast on the smooth glistening *piste*.

At first the others were not convinced and despondent at the thought of a further long haul, but it was evident we must move at once for the sun was high now and everywhere the snow ran with melt-water. We must cross the Fåbergstølsbre whilst the remaining snow-bridges were still solid. The going was good at first, though the sledge runners lay deep in the now slushy surface, but by midday we had reached the first crevasses and were forced to zigzag from side to side to detour impossible gaps. No more than ten yards of progress was possible between the slits and sometimes less than half the length of a sledge would fit on the ice-ledge between two fissures. There was no way of telling the depth of these gaping voids for they possessed no visible floors. The couloirs of firm ice between them were deceptive, only their centre line being safe; for the top layer of snow was undermined and threatened to break away under our weight, plunging us and the sledges into the dark frozen depths from which came a distant gurgle of subterranean waters.

Geoff, sweating profusely though his shirt was off, was harnessed to our sledge some six hundred metres ahead of the others. We came to a veritable maze of split ice with but thin bridges of rotten snow providing a way out.

Patrick had gone ahead and we were attempting to follow his spoor. He could not have realised how much heavier we were with the overloaded sledge: furthermore, he was still on skis which dispersed his weight, whereas we had been forced to remove ours to obtain sufficient leverage to pull the *půlks* in the gripping slush. Where his trail led, we could not always follow in safety and Geoff voiced my growing fears.

'If the crust should collapse, I'm going to be pulled down with the sledge and you wouldn't stand a dog's chance of finding me down one of those. We should have roped up before coming into this area.'

We waited until the others arrived. Even as I watched, Bob Powell gave a quick shout and fell through the crust up to his waist, plunging his axe deep into the snow ahead to arrest his fall. Henrik was frowning, but he and Roger disagreed that we should rope up at this stage, for they felt we would only find a way through the crevasse zone by maintaining speed of movement, by pulling the sledges as fast as possible over the snow-bridges with all hands at work pulling and pushing – rather than half the manpower to front and rear on safety ropes. Tempers were high with the strain of the work and the apprehension of impending disaster, but eventually it was agreed to fasten ropes to the rear of the sledges with roped 'anchormen' walking a hundred yards behind each *půlk*.

At any moment the rotten crust might give way but the ropes gave us a faint chance of recovering a sledge. The most unnerving job was that of the 'husky', for he was firmly strapped to the bamboo sledge-poles and, unlike the others, would stand no chance of flinging himself clear in the event of a fall. We had tried manoeuvring the *pulks* without use of the harnesses but they simply would not budge, being too heavy.

We became adept at spotting the weaker bridges and avoiding them even though it might mean a longish detour from our axis to find stronger crossing points. It was upsetting to find one's feet plunging through the crust from time to time, but so long as one quickly jack-knifed at the waist and dug one's ice-axe in firmly, there seemed little risk of whole bridges collapsing, for there had not been enough rain and unclouded sunshine since the last snowfall to undermine the main spines of the larger bridges.

By late afternoon we were a few hundred yards short of the rock cluster and pleased to find that, although a steep icy slope led up to it, there was a level patch of snow where the slope met the shelter of the rocks; an area just large enough to pitch our tents and store the equipment. But the men were exhausted, wanting only a meal and rest, and the last steep gradient was too much. Even with eight of us hauling with a concerted effort, we failed to move the *pulks*, so we unloaded them and wearily took the lighter items and skis up to the camp site. I found the Union Jack and climbed above the lower rocks to wedge it in a cranny above the tents.

We had arrived at the crucial point from whence, during the next four days, groups of two or three must find their way to a series of commanding points in the surrounding mountains. They would take radios and theodolites, fluorescent flags and fifteen-foot bamboo poles and establish inter-visible control points around the Fåbergstølsbre ice-tongue: thus setting up a framework for the survey map. This must be completed by the 21st of the month if we were to make use of the guides who would on that day be available to lead us over the glacier to Briksdal, a forty-kilometre journey through an intricate maze of ice-fields.

Once the local mists descended our control points would naturally be useless but, since the threatened low-pressure belt had not materialised and there were no signs of even localised hill mist, I felt we should press on at once to establish the three vital control points without which the rest of the survey programme would be a waste of time. Two of these points were in fact permanent

Norwegian trig points and probably marked by stone cairns. In this way we would relate our map to the existing charts.

Somewhere behind us to the north-east lay the icy bulge of the Fåbergstølsnøse, on the highest point of which lay a trig point at 1,554 metres.

Roger and Peter the geologist were to reach the *nøse*, or ice shoulder, by midday the following morning.

Henrik was to find a way through or around the crevasse-field we had just traversed and – again by twelve noon the next day – establish two points on the crest of the precipice which flanks the southern course of the ice-tongue. All these points must be so chosen as to be inter-visible and have a clear view of the top and bottom of the tongue. Henrik would be accompanied by Bob and Patrick carrying their radio and survey gear.

The third control – another Norwegian trig point – was not so simple for it lay well to the east of the ice-tongue and was not even part of the main Jostedals glacier. To reach it meant finding a way down to the valley, four thousand feet below, contacting the Land-Rover base camp set up by Johnnie Muir on a track near Öysaeter, and taking a theodolite, radio, and marker flares up a 5,000-foot gully. This entailed a difficult climb up a steep ravine to the east of Öysaeter but the position should be manned no later than the other two. Geoff, David and I decided to leave at once to find a route down by nightfall.

* * *

Lightly equipped, we reached the valley by dusk and soon found the Land-Rovers parked around tents and a wood fire. Johnnie, Brendan and the girls were pleased to see us and to hear there had been no serious accidents. Henrik had bound up my hand and Geoff's ribs the evening before. With much to do and plan it was easy to forget the throbbing ache, though Geoff had to be careful not to jolt his rib-cage when climbing.

We slept well that night and were loath to wake – well before dawn – to begin the ascent to Geoff's control point loaded up with theodolites, radio, marker flares and poles.

We came to the summit line after an eight-hour slog up the gully and, giving David the heavy radio as soon as we reached the level ground on top, I retraced the gully-trail back to the camp.

Above the first ice-fall of the Briksdalsbre.

The Briksdalsbre.

The day had been cloudless until midday when an ominous haze shrouded the sun and thunder rumbled from the south. I was tired having twice descended and once ascended four thousand feet in the last eighteen hours and rested for a while by the camp-fire listening to Johnnie's radios.

There was a Racal and a small A40 set and both were crackling away with messages from the unseen control points above. The groups had all arrived on time but were having difficulty sighting one another and were shooting off flares in an attempt to pinpoint each others' locations.

As one of our ice camp radios was useless after falling away from its parachute bundle, I must take a replacement and spare batteries back up to the ice camp-site before dark to give it to one of the groups. The sky was now overcast and a light rain falling, so I left with Johnnie who would help me over the difficult moraines which lead to the firm rock above the glacial snout.

We came to the blue cavern at the tip of the Fåbergstølsbre ice-tongue from where issues a torrent of pounding water in the manner of liquid fire from the mouth of some sinuous dragon. Here Brendan was squatting by a large boulder, having left the base camp early that morning. He had erected a 15-foot-high triangle of bamboos with coloured bunting flapping from its apex; he was trying to speak over his radio but the air was occupied; angry voices buzzing through the static.

There was a heated exchange between Roger and Geoff – the supervisor of the survey programme – as to the exact location of their respective positions. Glancing up, I was not surprised. Sheer cliffs reared above us to the north and south, their upper slopes invisible in swirling swathes of mist. To the west the frozen river with its multiple dark scars rose silently within its containing cliffs to melt with the grey sky; an opaque and invisible rendezvous of ice and obscuring vapour, an amorphous meeting place of the clammy elements indefinable to the eye.

The radio was silent for a while then Roger's voice came through clearly as though he stood beside us, not many hundreds of feet above; higher even than the mist. His tones were frustrated for Henrik's team could see his point whilst he and Peter could not see them.

'You must be blind,' radioed Patrick, 'we have erected our

marker on a back-bearing of four thousand mils from your position. We are also about two hundred metres below the edge of the summit-ice.'

Johnnie and I left Brendan. I presumed that the survey groups had taken their tents and rations with them and would hardly try to move back to the ice camp now that the mists had set in on top. The thunder was continuous and closer as we stumbled amongst the loose boulders of the sheer moraines. Once on to the firmer rock of the cliffs above the ice-tongue, Johnnie left me, and I continued slowly up the slippery face traversing above the ice-tongue until a low re-entrant, with roaring waterfall pouring over the lips of its entrance, led the way to a desolate valley which rose in a series of crumbling buttresses to the ice-cap of the main glacier. Somewhere up there lay the ice camp, now swathed in mist and driving sleet. The whole of this valley was awash, glittering streaks pouring down from its icy fringe to join the central torrent. Ankle-high water rushed wherever I trod and an unreasonable fear lay at the back of my mind causing a nagging urge to climb, to get above this alarming deluge and away from the overall growing roar of the rising waters.

By eight o'clock I came to the level of the ice, soaked and shivering, for the wind blew from the ice-plateau carrying with it a stinging sleet. Twice I had taken a bad route up the final buttress and been forced down again. The weight of water pouring over the buttress made it difficult to see a reasonable route and the heavy rucksack did not help matters. Being no glaciologist, I could not understand why, when it was so cold, the sleet and rain did not turn to snow, nor why it did not freeze solid on contact with the ice. True it was August and the hottest period of the year, but the temperature appeared to me to be below freezing. I could only presume, as I watched the white tongues of water gushing from the ice-plateau, that the air above the ice was affected by warmer currents from the valley below and that there was just too great a volume of water racing down too quickly for it to freeze.

Worried, for exposure can set in unexpectedly in such conditions, I had moved across to the southern edge of the buttress where it met the ice-tongue – though separated from it by a formidable gap – and ascended a steep but firm route without the rucksack, hauling it up after me with a hundred-foot length of nylon rope.

The thought of warm tent and dry sleeping-bag kept my legs moving, but cautiously, for visibility was low and I was lost. After visiting numerous possible outcrops leading on to the ice, desperation was in the offing – as no doubt was pneumonia – when I stumbled on the Union Jack lying in a pool. I picked it up and climbed into the wind over a jumble of metamorphic rock. Suddenly the ice-rim and the tents were before me but my relief was tempered by anxiety for the others. I did not call out, for it was painfully obvious they were absent.

Everywhere lay sodden equipment. The tents were on their sides in pools of melt-water. Sleeping-bags, radios, skis and ration packs were strewn about as though abandoned in a hurry. Clothes and ski-boots lay quite far from the tents – blown there perhaps by the gale before they became waterlogged. Even the level snow-patch was no longer; now just a sloping grey layer of mush.

Geoff and David would be all right, for there was little or no ice where I had left them that morning and they could find their way back to the gully, but what of Roger and Peter some six kilometres over the ice on the Fåbergstølsnøse? And Henrik's group on the far side of the ice-tongue and crevasse-field?

For some unfathomable reason they had taken none of the tents, nor any sleeping-bags or rations. Even a tourist visiting these parts must take full protection from the elements. Both Henrik and Roger were experienced enough to know better than to venture into the ice-fields carrying no means of protection. The temperature was well below freezing point and the violent blizzard would lower the body's defences even more rapidly than the low temperature.

There was a single strip of damp snow at the uppermost lip of the ice-field and I moved the tents there one by one, cursing as they persistently blew away from my numb grasp. Grabbing sleeping-bags and clothes, I passed them through the entrance-holes knowing this to be of little use for they were thoroughly drenched. I could see perhaps five yards into the gloom and shouted hoarsely; my voice being carried away like a jinking feather in the gale. I found the emergency flares and fired some into the mist. There was no reply as I listened intently – save my own teeth chattering, the hiss of moving melt-water and the wind.

SIX

Moving Ice

COULD THEY HAVE BECOME lost in the blizzard and fallen over a cliff or into a crevasse? It was possible. I tried to reject such thoughts and clambered into one of the little tents. Once in the damp comfort of my sleeping-bag I switched on the A40 radio, calling again and again, but no reply came. I left the radio switched on and lay listening to its buzz and the rustle of my legs twitching in the cold wet bag. Perhaps I should try to find my way down to the valley and alert a search party. On reflection this seemed pointless, for no effective group could be mustered before noon the following day at best, and if the lost men survived till dawn they would be able to make their own way back to the ice camp, or anyway to inform me of their plight on a radio.

These A40s were effective over a couple of miles in such conditions only if there was no mountain mass between the two sets. Therefore I must remain where I was in case either group had a distress message to send. To wander off into the blizzard in the blind hope of running into them – and not into a crevasse – seemed a useless course.

The events of that evening might well have proved tragic; as it was, the survey groups experienced a night they would never forget, a journey which might well have been dreamed up by Hammond Innes – for the elements beggared all but his most vivid descriptions of a frozen hell on earth. Rather than relate a second-hand account, I have extracted passages from the personal diaries of those involved. These suffer possibly from understatement, but will enjoy the sympathy of the reader who has experienced that panic and blind fear which comes from being lost in a strange land – let alone in a dark frozen world of rushing water and yawning fissures where a false step in the all-obscuring mist might lead over an abyss.

I have intermingled extracts from the diaries of Roger and Peter:

> No sooner had Peter and I dismantled the theodolite than the mist surrounded us. It just enveloped us bringing with it sleet and driving rain. Then it dawned on us, the stupid mistake we had made. The golden rule in such mountains when a mist descends is to stay where you are, erect a tent, and crawl into your sleeping-bag until the mist lifts. As the weather had been glorious when we left ice camp that morning and the weight of the survey kit, theodolite and radio had been back-breaking, we had dispensed with both tent and sleeping bags. How stupid we were! There was naught for it but to attempt to reach the safety and warmth of ice camp, but there was one large snag. Between us and ice camp, on the direct route we had come by, lay a 600-foot gorge. There was, however, an eight-kilometre ice-traverse which flanked this gorge.
>
> It was worth a chance for even if we huddled together under a rock for warmth, we would only have a small chance of survival in this bitter howling wind.

> . . . it was becoming late – we tried to locate Patrick's position again, but without joy. Cloud was moving up from the valley: visibility, never very good that evening, became worse, making any further searching a waste of time. At about 1800 hours Roger and I put the equipment behind a large boulder and set off. The mist and growing gale soon cut visibility to a few yards so, once on the ice, we moved on a compass course and counted our steps. It was difficult to pace accurately because from time

to time we had to climb over outcrops of slippery rock, but the effort was eventually justified.

Heading into the blizzard was an almost ethereal experience: masses of rock would loom out of the cloud, at first seeming to be very distant and then appearing in detail only a few yards away.

The surface of the glacier itself was melting at an unbelievable rate.

Where the ice was level we walked through slush and rotten ice with water well above our ankles. Where there was a slope, black streams had formed which rushed past at torrential speeds. One such temporary hazard was especially impressive, not for its size but for the velocity of the water hurtling down it. Although only a yard across and about two feet deep, it moved so fast that to have slipped and fallen in would have meant being carried down into the unseen valley below.

. . . we slithered and fell on the ice sometimes disappearing up to our thighs in glacial streams which flowed across the ice-field. No, it was far from pleasant. Peter noticed a couple of drowned lemmings in the centre of an ice-field which he felt was significant. I tried not to share his view.

According to my calculations we should have reached ice camp by about 2015 hours, but as this hour came up, all we could see through stinging eyes was mist and ice. We could not tell whether it went up or went down. My heart beat a little faster. Oh my God, have I made a mistake in my calculations? If so, then we are in deep trouble.

At 2030 hours we hit rock which appeared to be running in the right direction so we left the compass-bearing and edged our way carefully down the rim of the rock. At least, if we had to stay out for the night, the rock might afford us some protection from the frozen tearing sleet.

. . . the clouds cleared for a moment to our right and through the gloom a pool of the most pure and startling blue I have ever seen appeared in the ice. It was almost thirty yards in diameter and lay but a short distance from us. In the grey monochrome of moving cloud, rock and ice, the purity and quality of the blue was breath-taking in its intensity. Then the mists closed in and it was gone as though but a mirage.

Without crampons, walking on the sloping, moving ice in rubber-soled boots was not easy. We did not dare to rope ourselves together for – if one of us fell – the other could not have held him and both of us would have slid over the edge together. We could not tell where the terminal rim of the ice lay, though the wet crunch of our boots was drowned by the background roar of water pouring off the glacier.

Roger felt we might be walking around the wrong outcrop – perhaps we had gone too far north and were in the middle of the main glacier; having seen the force of the water melting off the ice, I wondered whether the camp had not been completely washed away. Even if it had not, we might miss it in the mist for the successive outcrops of rock were most confusing. Each successive bay in the rock-piles looked like the one with the camp.

By now finding the camp was the be-all and end-all of our lives. To sleep in a tent with a sleeping-bag, no matter how wet, seemed the ultimate luxury. We wanted nothing more than that, and did not think further.

. . . suddenly Peter pointed to the front and I quickened my pace. 'That's it, I'm sure that's it!' he shouted against the wind. I could not see anything in the swirling mist. 'Are you sure?' I asked with my heart pounding. 'Yes, I can see the tents.' We ran the last few yards into the camp in our relief.

We were numb with cold and awkwardly stripped off one another's clothes, climbed into the tent where Ran was, and crawled into one sleeping-bag so that the meagre warmth from our huddled bodies could warm each other's frozen limbs. Both of us had uncontrollable shivers and Ran produced a flask of brandy. It tasted good as it burnt its way down my throat then swelled up with heat in my stomach.

'Have you heard anything of Henrik's group?' I asked Ran.

'No, I've been trying to get them on the radio, but there's no answer.'

'They can't possibly have tried to cross the crevasse field: not in this blizzard,' said Peter, 'it would be suicidal.'

As I lay trying to control my shivering limbs, I tried to put my mind into that of Henrik's. What had he done? Were they now trying to cross the crevasse-field, roped up and following the flickering luminosity of a compass needle? One slip in the night, with this driving sleet and mist, would be disastrous: whoever was on the end of the rope might not be able to react quickly enough with numbed senses to check the fall of the others. Even if he did, he would not have a chance in hell of pulling them up the side of those ninety-foot deep crevasses; so sheer, wet and insecure.

Outside the wind was trying its utmost to tear our tent from its secure position. The canvas slapped unceasingly as the wind howled its crescendo of agony. I do not envy them.

* * *

Relieved as I was at the arrival of Peter and Roger, I noticed their poor state which did not bode well for the other group. They had crossed over no crevassed ground, however slippery and sheer their route, whereas Henrik's team must pass right across the rotten snow of the moving ice-tongue, dangerous enough in daylight. Both Roger and Peter were having difficulty in speaking and, though obviously exhausted, they were shivering convulsively, unable to sleep. Their skin was a mottled green in the torchlight, their lips cracked, and icy particles of sleet clung to their hair. They lay together shuddering and sucking numb fingers. Quite why the glacier was melting at so furious a rate when the temperature was so low eluded me, but the Jostedal was both unpredictable and inexplicable at the best of times.

All of us must on past occasions have spent nights out in bad weather with only a rock for protection, and thought little of it. But here we were well over five thousand feet above sea-level and we were experiencing hostile elements such as we had not encountered before. Between the survey points and our tents there was no cover but the scattered rock outcrops which were lashed from every side by the howling gale and stinging sleet. We all wore 'waterproof' anoraks, normally effective, but even these were soon sodden by the torrential and horizontally blown ice particles. They dissolved on contact to pour down the neck and legs.

Furthermore, the rocks were alive with running water and the ice-crust was no more than a mobile slush.

The fittest of us would not last long in such conditions for the high wind-speed over so wet and icy an area was more lethal than far colder surroundings where one could find a modicum of shelter to preserve the body's inner warmth.

The frequency of strong winds in the proximity of the Jostedal makes this region more adverse to human activity than the very much colder regions farther north, because, from the point of view of human comfort, the increased mean wind-speed more than offsets the accompanying higher temperatures.

I listened to the sinister song of the Jostedal giving vent to a cacophony of violence, an orchestra of cruel beauty with the all-pervading wind providing demon flute and clarion. The vicious hiss of driven sleet lashing rock rose and fell – muted cymbals preparing the ear for the numbing fortissimo of the drum – a cavernous roar of falling water that plucked at the nerves. Here was an overture fit for Armageddon, and I shuddered to think of our three companions groping through the dark and hostile auditorium that lay outside the relative but sufficient protection of our tents.

Henrik and Patrick kept no record of their experiences that night: the following is taken from Bob Powell's matter-of-fact personal notes written shortly after his return to Newcastle:

> Time was slipping by as we sought to close our control point. Geoff radioed at 1730 hours to say he was worried, for a mist was slowly filling the valley below his position and ominous black thunder-clouds were rolling in from the south. By 1800 hours the clouds were also evident to us, the light began to fade, and conditions deteriorated rapidly. We decided to return to ice camp with haste.
>
> Thirty minutes later we were in sight of the edge of the ice tongue but by then conditions were appalling. Rain lashed the rock and our route back lay wreathed in mist. The prospect of traversing the tongue was not inviting.
>
> After a hurried discussion, we decided to try to get down to the valley below rather than risk the ice and so moved down the rock parallel with the glacial snout. Farther down, the snout

looked safer and we tried to cross over on to its ice. Twice we were able to get within forty feet of a possible crossing place, but each time the final pitch was too steep.

Reflecting on our plight, I realised we had fallen into a common trap; the day had earlier seemed bright and clear so we had left without protection kit or adequate rations. Now, in a blizzard, we faced the prospect of huddling together under our three groundsheets or the equally unpleasant alternative of a blind traverse of the Fåbergstølsbre crevasse-field.

What followed was not exactly an argument; we were far too cold and worried to waste time arguing, but – whereas I favoured finding some form of shelter – Patrick was adamant that, with no tent in the freezing wind, we must attempt the crossing. Henrik was undecided but, swayed by our lack of food or dry clothes, agreed with Patrick and the decision was made.

The next four hours were an unforgettable hell. The earlier sledge crossing of the area had been a picnic by comparison since we had then been able to see the dangers: now they were obscured and increased, for the driving rain had melted all but a few of the remaining snow-bridges and those that still existed were rotten and difficult to find in the gloom.

I began to suffer from stomach-ache – the result perhaps of drinking ice-water which, because it contains no minerals, runs straight through one's system. I could not stop to rest as the cold was biting into all of us and we must plod on like robots.

It is easy not to be nervous when you are frozen stiff and crave only for warmth.

I followed only the black line of the rope as Henrik, leading with his compass, was hidden in the misty gloom. God knows how he managed to sort out any useful bearing from his compass – we were spending more time detouring the black lips of crevasses than heading in any particular direction. I had long since lost any sense of orientation.

It must have been near midnight when I noticed a steep rising pitch ahead. Could this be the final gradient? We paused to shout. No answer; perhaps the others were in similar difficulties. Another hundred metres with the slope increasing and again we stopped to shout. This time there came a faint answering cry followed by the refracted glimmer of a torch. This was nearly our downfall, for as we turned, elated and quickened our pace, Henrik plunged through a snow-bridge to his armpits. Caution was still required and it took fifteen frustrating minutes to negotiate the last hundred metres of the slippery gradient.

Peter, Ran and Roger were in one tent. We climbed exhausted into another. Everything was wet but at least the wind could no longer cut into us. We polished off a half bottle of whisky between us, and Henrik climbed into a sleeping-bag with me. I shivered uncontrollably for the five hours before dawn; decidedly the most miserable night of my life.

* * *

The effort to leave our tents on the morrow was considerable, but the gale had died down and though the mists were still thick and the air clammy, at least we had respite from the wind and rain.

Four of the team, though game to carry on the programme, looked poorly and shivered continuously, so we agreed to shelve the survey schedule for a day's rest and recuperation in which to dry out the clothes and ourselves.

Apart from diagnosing mild doses of exposure, Henrik was worried about Bob's and his own lips which were severely cracked and bled freely when they talked or ate. He delved into his comprehensive medical pack and, after deliberation, produced a tube of pink cream.

'This is most wonderful stuff for the lips when the weather is like now. Bob, we will put some on and you will see. By tonight your lips will be better; in two days – back to normal! This ointment is supplied only to the Finnish Army.'

We were lucky that day for the clouds dispersed, followed by hot sunshine and a light breeze in which to dry out the clothes and sleeping-bags. We ate well – double the allotted rations from the highly calorised 'commando' packs with hourly brews of whisky-laced tea.

But time was not a commodity to waste: already we had lost the day gained by jumping on the 12th. Geoff had returned safely to the base camp and radioed plans for future deployment of the survey teams. Early the next day, the groups were to return to their previous locations but this time fully equipped for a three-day period. In this manner we hoped the sightings could be completed whenever the weather allowed. Peter agreed to curtail his own geological programme for Roger needed his help.

Meanwhile in the valley below, Norris Riley the glaciologist had arrived from Sweden and set out with Johnnie and Brendan to begin his glaciological research at the base of the ice-snout. He carried with him a number of poles and accessories including a seven-foot-long hollow drill to bore holes of over a metre into various parts of the snout. Norris had lost the sight of one eye but felt at home on the ice, hopping around on the snout no matter how fissured the area of his research.

Brendan's work was painstaking and detailed. At first he had aided Johnnie with the radio network; then for four days he left the base camp for the ice-plateau, carrying with him his own private laboratory. Realising the difficulties of the terrain through an earlier journey to the Jostedal, he had come well prepared – not with the usual bulky trappings of the field biologist, cumbersome Berlese funnels and glass containers, but simply with a large number of self-sealing plastic bags. His method was obviously successful, for his collection – now in the British Museum – numbers some 1,771 specimens of Collembola from over thirty differing species and includes a species hitherto unknown in Norway. At the end of the four days he descended from the ice and arrived overjoyed at the base camp to show Johnnie and Norris his magnificent collection.

They looked hard and long into the little bags of lichen, mud, sphagnum and even tree bark, but found it difficult to share Brendan's enthusiasm for, try as they would, they could see positively no sign of life amongst the various samples.

This was not surprising for Brendan's entire programme, carried out on the nunataks of the ice-cap itself, in the Fåberg valley to the east, and the Briksdal valley to the west, was devoted to a population study of one of the world's smallest wingless insects – the Collembola.

Although sparse research has been carried out on Collembola, also known as Springtails, they in fact form a major section of the entire insect world and are to be found almost anywhere from the Arctic to the Antarctic. Unlike most other organisms, they are not unduly worried by temperature changes so that a particular subspecies might be found on mountain ranges or in the depths of caves and from snow-line to shore-line. Collembola are most important to man for they feed on dead plant material, increase soil aeration and thus the surface area available to nitrifying bacteria. This results in an overall increase in soil fertility.

However, the balance of nature is not too difficult to upset: recently a herbiverous species of Springtail with localised populations in the general area of the Jostedals Glacier was accidentally introduced into Australia.

In a very short time it has become a serious pest there since it consumes large quantities of lucerne, thus having a deleterious effect on the number of sheep grazed per acre – in severe cases with as much as a seventy-five per cent reduction. This shows too that a Springtail used to a cool temperate climate can thrive in a sub-tropical area, and, since its natural predators would not have been simultaneously introduced to the new habitat, it would gain an almost unchecked reproduction potential.

Little effective control of these 'mini-monsters' can be estab-lised until we know far more about their biology and the complex structure of their micro-habitats in relation to the total eco-system, and Brendan was certainly doing his bit for science during his two weeks 'worm-hunt' (as Johnnie described his energetic grovellings in the ice, alluvial mud and moraine dust).

For three days of mist and drizzle the survey groups moved around the system of control points and by noon on the 18th had completed the many hundreds of separate sightings required. The work was cold and boring but one could not slacken concentration since even the slightest slips might render the resulting figures unacceptable when it came to evaluation.

With Roger and Peter, I moved along the rocks to ice camp to deposit the theodolite and heavy tripod by the sledges. We would have lunch and then move down on to the ice-tongue itself with bundles of survey poles and metal stakes. A sledge-hammer too – which alone weighed over twenty pounds.

For a while we sat idly watching some of the others on the glacier, threading their way through the ice like five ants on a wedding cake. Peter reflected that the whole area was of great interest to geologists and he was determined to come back some other time if the survey schedule hindered his researches now.

As far as Peter could make out the whole Fåberg area must lie on a bedrock of complex gneisses formed during the Caledonian orogeny and these had then undergone several stages of metamorphism. He pointed down to the northern rock flank of the snout where it was possible to pick out such strange structures as banding, folding, augen gneiss, extreme metamorphism and zones of mineralisation. The whole face looked like some modern art painting for some of the more coherent beds had become contorted into tight folds of extreme complexity under high temperatures and pressures.

The overall topography of the valley rock must have been established during the last four quaternary ice-ages and today's glaciers flowed in valleys formed by older, earlier, glacial advances. As a whole the glacier was in general retreat for you could see the huge boulders left behind by the ice all along the floor of the valley bottom. However, during this overall movement of retreat there could be minor advances, depending on how the amount of ablation or melting compared with the annual snow accumulation. Every year differed and if our map was a success it would show exactly what the ice had done during the last decade.

Munching a solid oatmeal block, Roger reflected how very intransitory and ineffective Man was when seen against so massive, so eternal an element as the glacier. The blue-white mass below us had contemplated the heavens for aeons of time and doubtless would continue to do so for countless years to come. The spirit of the ice must laugh to itself to see our puny efforts at recording its movement, its shape and its nature. In a while it will change absolutely and our records will soon be outdated. The ice will continue to alter when we are long since dead, like the lemmings frozen for centuries in its icy veneer.

Peter felt that the glacier was melting fast at the present moment but did not know whether it was melting at the same rate as other European glaciers, nor how its speed compared with the retreat of the Polar ice-caps. It was a sobering thought that all this meltwater was pouring into the oceans for it would need only a one-metre rise in the ocean's level for catastrophic floods to occur on every coastline.

I pictured for a moment the entire Jostedalsbre as a giant bath and tried to get a mental image of the amount of water which might be released should our solar system alter but slightly for the warmer. It was not easy to visualise this for what a vast bath six hundred square kilometres of solid ice with a depth varying from three to six hundred metres would make.

It was not necessary to imagine a plug for this bath for the plateau already had twenty-four glaciers flowing from it. Twenty-four frozen rivers each moving infinitely slowly through deep valleys down to the fjords. These frozen rivers also formed the only icy highways on to this mountain fortress: sitting above the formidable Fåbergstølsbre, one of the gentlest of these ice-arms, I wondered what the notorious Briksdalsbre would look like seen from above.

If our survey programme could be finished by the following day, we were to meet two local glacier guides at our ice camp. With skis and sledges we would follow them over successive curving ice-fields for more than forty kilometres to our 'escape' route by the Briksdalsbre, since we could not leave by the way we had come. Inge Lødøen, the Norwegian Tourist Director at Stryn had warned me to have a tent and food ready for the guides. They would come from the north, he had said, by way of the distant Bödalsaeter track and so carry no rucksacks. When I had asked Mr. Lødøen if this were wise; they might get lost after all, or bad weather might catch them before they reached us, he had merely chuckled.

He had said that men such as David Mindresunde and Jan Mickelbust never got lost on the *bre*. No one knew the Jostedalsbre as well as David did for he had even lived up there at the start of the last war when a German invasion was expected. Evidently the Norwegians had feared that the Germans might try to land on the plateau by parachute, but they never did.

I was looking forward to meeting these guides. I have never met a people more likeable than the Norwegians: there is something of the dour but trusty Scot about them, enlivened by a simple humour and zest for life. Proud and independent yet immensely generous, they seem to take great pleasure in their kindness to strangers, indeed hospitality seems almost to be a duty of life with them as it is with the Arabs.

During the descent of the Briksdalsbre.

Seen through a telescopic lens, two of the ice team appear briefly on the plateau between the third and fourth ice-falls of the Briksdalsbre. The area of the *bergschrund* lies between the rock and the ice.

Then too, everyone likes to be liked, and the Norwegians on the whole seem to have time for the British. Most of them speak English and many have spent holidays in England or Scotland. On past visits I had met only a few farmers and older fisherfolk who knew no English, so it came as a surprise later to find that neither of our appointed guides could speak anything but Norwegian.

We finished our snack, shouldered the packs and moved off.

Three hours later we approached the others on the frozen tongue. They were in two groups, their orange anoraks visible from afar as they moved from hummock to hummock with the long survey poles.

Geoff was commanding activities over a small radio and, following the well spread-out line of orange blobs from his position near the neck of the ice-tongue, I saw the ragged line of poles – red, white and black – running right down the spine of the glacial snout. The sticks were wooden and were only held in place by wire lashing them to sharp metal angle-irons. From the cliffs to either side came the resonant echo of climbing-hammers thudding on metal as the irons were driven into the ice.

Grey runnels marked the ice where the melt-water of decades had rushed by. Here the surface was so hard that even our crampon-spikes made no impression. It was heavy work driving the irons in, even with Roger's sledge-hammer.

That afternoon, nearing the base of the snout, we saw a small group of shirtless climbers wending their way up the ice. Three were tough-looking men with ropes and ice-axes, the fourth was a young woman, blonde hair tucked up beneath a peaked cap.

All work came to a grinding halt, poles were dropped, and the eight of us stood silently, rudely watching. The girl was very pretty, well tanned like the men she was following except for her breasts which swung free as she walked: they were as white as the ice. Like a fool I had not brought a telescopic lens for the Nikkon, but on reflection perhaps *The Sunday Times* would not appreciate evidence of this sort of expedition highlight.

The vision passed on up the glacier, and we heaved a communal sigh.

The poles were completed; planted at 200-metre intervals over a two-kilometre stretch of ice. Now Geoff moved upwards with half the team: they would collect the subtense-bar at the top of the pegged stretch and work slowly downwards. The others – using a theodolite and sixteen-feet-long measured staves – would work upwards from the snout to complete a tacheometric traverse which would give us accurate readings of the complex contour lines of the ice-tongue.

But the gloom of dusk came early to our deep ravine, forcing us to postpone further sightings until the next day.

Rejoining Geoff's group we heard their disheartening news. The ice surface had not settled down yet – after the recent rapid ablation – with an unforseen result.

As the 360-degree sightings were taken, the 'target' poles were moving very slightly with the overall motion of the surface ice. In itself a minute change of position, it was enough to make the recorded sightings totally unacceptable.

There was nothing we could do but return the next day in the hope that the glacier would settle down.

I prayed hard that night that all would be well with the ice. If not, we would miss the guides. They would not wait and I dreaded the thought of the ice-crossing and descent without them.

* * *

Up before dawn, we were back on the ice-spine at first light. Working with Roger, I heard Geoff's radio call from above.

'The ice movement is negligible now. I'm getting good readings with acceptable margins of error. But would you believe it – the survey poles have all popped out like champagne corks during the night!'

So, like a family of woodpeckers, we were back to work with the hammers and stakes, replacing the poles which had slid into deep crevasses and re-sighting others where the ice was too hard to take the iron pegs.

Geoff pointed to a deep cavity in the ice where a pole had been. 'That was not there yesterday. Let's hope no more craters open up while we're here.'

Inge Lødøen had told me a strange story of the Bödalsbre, a glacier to the west of us, where village children had recently found a corpse. Police visited the spot and found – at the very end of the snout by a newly opened fissure – the perfectly preserved body of an old man dressed in the style of clothes worn by local shepherds four hundred years earlier.

I glanced into Geoff's newly-found crevasse but if there was a body there it was not to be seen, for there was no visible bottom to the crack, just a faint gurgle of water from far below.

By midday both groups had completed their areas and we said goodbye to Peter and David. They were to find their own way down to the valley and base camp. Peter was to catch up on his geological work; David had to leave us for he was due in Kenya later that week. They took with them the important survey notebooks, the most delicate of the survey equipment and some of the charts.

Had the terrain allowed we could have followed them down to the valley then and there, for the survey was complete; but many porters would be needed, and many hours of good weather, if we were to get the heavy and more bulky equipment carried down the precipitous tracks to the valley five thousand feet below.

All being well we would be at the base of the Briksdal ice-arm in two days' time. From its very foot we would reach the roadside below in our rubber boats. No porters, no sweat.

The plan was reasonable if ambitious. There was sufficient rope – some 1600 feet in all – to see us down the Briksdalsbre however steep and treacherous its ice-falls might prove. All the team now had some conception of ice conditions and so should have an idea of what to expect. I explained that if anyone wished to leave with Peter and David, he could depart with a clear conscience, knowing that all the survey work was done. No one commented; all seemed to be looking forward to seeing and, if possible, descending the notorious Briksdalsbre about which we had heard so much.

SEVEN

A World of Mists

WE CAME TO THE ice camp as the first stars glinted above and twinkling lights beckoned from distant Fåberg – I shivered thinking of warmth and dry comforts.

The guides should arrive soon. Bödal lay to the north-west and I scanned the icy expanse to the right of Lodalskapa with binoculars. A light drizzle fell and lurking mists moved across the plateau.

By nine o'clock it was almost too dark for safe movement on the ice.

Roger was worried, 'Perhaps they have not set off because of the conditions or have returned to the Bödal valley. It's very wet tonight and after all they've no tents or food.'

'If they don't make it tonight, they never will,' I replied 'for Mr. Lødøen stressed they could only spare two days away from their normal jobs.'

I glanced away from the Bödal; something was moving along the rim of the Fåberg crevasse-field. Then it was gone; the only movement being the black slits of the fissures exposed and then hidden again by the creeping tendrils of mist. Quite suddenly a wind current, spiralling off the cold face, sucked a mist patch with it and exposed two figures moving slowly up the slope.

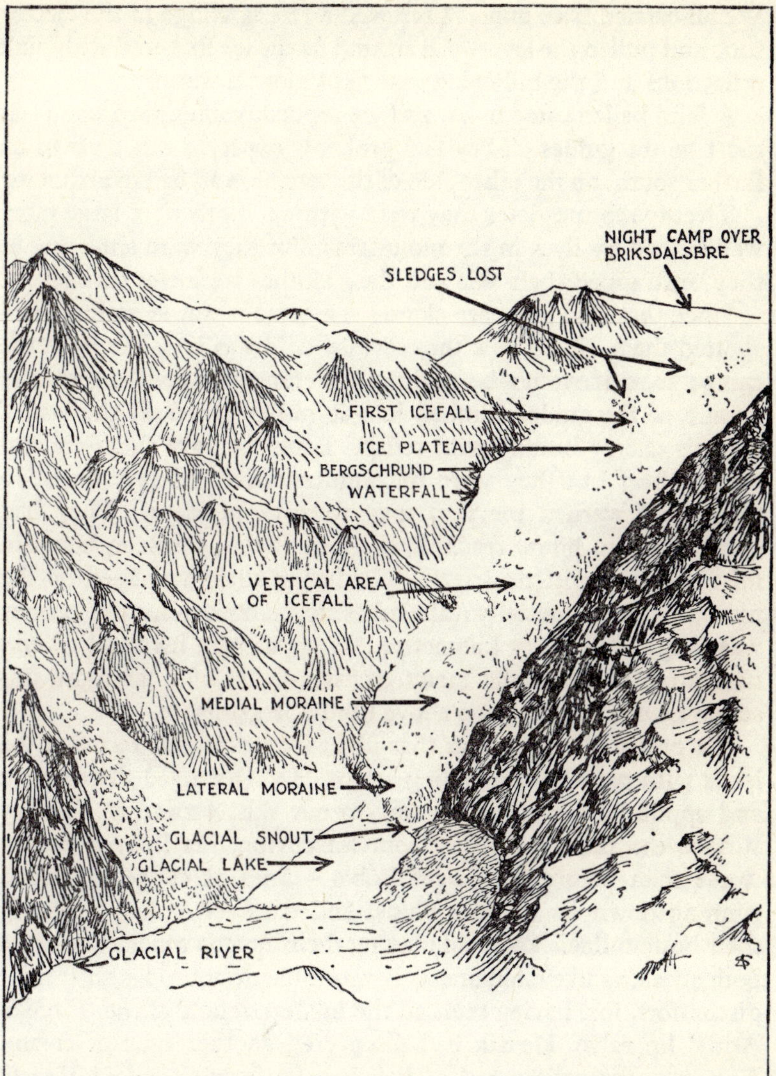
NIGHT CAMP OVER
BRIKSDALSBRE
SLEDGES. LOST
FIRST ICEFALL
ICE PLATEAU
BERGSCHRUND
WATERFALL
VERTICAL AREA
OF ICEFALL
MEDIAL MORAINE
LATERAL MORAINE
GLACIAL SNOUT
GLACIAL LAKE
GLACIAL RIVER

The ice-fall

We all carried flare guns. I screwed a red cartridge to the ejector tube and pulled the lever. All around us the ice flickered with pink reflections and the billowing tent-flaps glowed warmly.

A faint halloa came to us, and we replied, yelling fortissimo – it must be the guides. They had probably expected our tents to be farther south, on the other side of the tongue, and had overshot us.

Twenty minutes later they were with us. Both were large men, well tanned by lives in the mountains, but they were shivering as they unstrapped their skis and their clothes were wet through.

Since they had no spare clothes nor tents it was as well we had spotted them. Even now the crevasse-field was invisible from the camp; soon it would be nightfall. Peter and David's tent was vacant, so the guides climbed into it and polished off the last of Roger's cherry brandy with relish. Later we gave them tea and curried beef but they were uncommunicative. Henrik spoke to them, and warned me that they were despondent. They had spent fourteen hours reaching us from Bödal; fourteen hours in mist and intermittent drizzle. Neither of them was keen on the morrow's task, especially if the mists stayed down – for the journey was long; some forty kilometres. It apparently involved careful navigation to avoid the many crevasse-fields of a far more unstable nature than the one above the Fåbergstølsbre.

We prepared the sledges that night by torchlight, securing the loads with parachute retaining-straps. Henrik gauged the weather and applied a sticky purple wax to our skis, expecting a slushy surface the next day. Far from improving, his lips were now worse than before – as were Bob's – lines of congealed blood running down on to their chins, and dark red cracks adorning their bottom lips. To avoid moving their lips too much, they were both speaking like Chinamen. It was difficult not to laugh at their discomfort, for, having realised the ineffectiveness of the 'Finnish Army' lip salve, Henrik had discovered another tube of cream. This one was yellow and of Polish manufacture. Again Henrik was effusive in his praise of its excellence, and they had both applied it liberally to their cracked skin. The next morning had found them in considerable pain so someone had produced a Boots' brand of common vaseline. From then on, as Henrik grudgingly admitted, their lips had begun to recover.

Geoff woke me at four o'clock the next morning and my glance through the entrance-hole was greeted by a thick clammy mist. Visibility was lower than ever before and yesterday's drizzle continued unabated. We had slept soundly, and ate an ample breakfast before taking down the tents – and the Union Jack. There was no room to stack them on the sledges so they were added to personal rucksacks much to the owners' displeasure.

Henrik had been talking to our guides as they dismantled their tent. He came over to tell us their ultimatum. It came as a shock for it was so unexpected and – as far as I could see – unwarranted.

Henrik's diary records their feelings:

> . . . Having spent a cold, wet and uncomfortable night our Norwegian guides were not in their best mood. We had lengthy discussions with them and I acted as translator. They advised us not to proceed with the Briksdal descent because of the weather conditions. They emphasised the danger in the form of deep crevasses.

Personally I gave the Norwegians right. Having, so to say, added up my own experiences of climbing – in ice and rocks in the Alps, Lapland, Africa and the Himalayas – I made a preliminary decision not to do the descent. The following factors were the most important ones:

1. Weather conditions plus the state of the glacier – it was the maximum melting period with danger of avalanches.
2. Poor equipment, i.e. no ice ladders, no special ice nails.
3. Lack of experience in ice. Having had some experience myself, it was still four years since my last glacier visit. None of the other members was experienced.
4. A similar opinion was expressed by the Norwegian guides...

But at the time Henrik was not so specific. He said only that the guides had spent a poor night in their wet clothes and – after their long trek the day before – they were not prepared to take us, in dangerously thick mists, on such a long journey.

Furthermore, they had seen Bob and Patrick trying to pull one of the loaded sledges up the fairly steep slope above the camp-site. They hadn't managed to budge it an inch.

On langlauf skis with a light rucksack, they said the distance would take eight hours to cover. Pulling these sledges, they estimated, we would spend at least two days over the journey, if in fact we could move them at all over the rougher stretches.

If only we had parachuted four husky dogs with the equipment!

I strained my eyes into the mists looking for a lighter more diffuse patch but there was none – it would be folly to set off without guides. We had maps but they showed none of the crevasse zones nor, and this was of greater importance, did they indicate the icy 'spine' which runs the length of the Jostedal with minimum rise and fall. By sticking to this ridge we could keep away from the undulating slopes which are so hard to detect and avoid; everything being white with no shadows to give perspective to the terrain. Any climb would be crippling with the overloaded sledges, but, if the guides would keep us to the 'spine' we should meet no further steep gradients once the first major haul from ice camp to plateau was achieved. They must come with us. I knew David Mindresunde had been well paid by the Tourist Association and that, since he knew the glaciers better than any other living man, his reputation as a guide would be partly at stake if he refused to lead us.

Roger, seeing that I was annoyed at the turn of events, stopped me from haranguing the guides and suggested we try diplomacy before threats and denouncement.

He and Bob prepared a thick gruel which they described as oxtail soup – though it neither looked like soup nor smelled like oxtail. Jan and David looked less sullen after it. The ensuing supplement of Mars bars, biscuits and cigarettes improved their mien yet further.

Perhaps their sit-down strike could be eased to a 'go-slow' now. I squatted by them in the slush with Henrik to translate.

'Did you enjoy the soup?'

'Yes.'

'Did you sleep O.K. last night?'

'No.'

An awkward silence.

'You agree that the mists may well lift later today and the going will be swift?'

'With those sledges of yours the going will be slow – mist or no mist,' muttered Jan.

'But everyone knows you are the best guide in Jotunheim,' I was addressing David, 'and the British and Norwegian television-men and journalists will be waiting below the Briksdal. We must not disappoint them and all the Norwegians who have helped to make the expedition possible. Now we have reached this stage, we cannot simply abandon all the equipment here because of a mere mist. We cannot hope to lower the sledges down the Fåberg arm but at Briksdal there will be a strong chance that we can. Surely you can see that?'

But David was adamant despite my cajoling; despite the 'oxtail' brew.

'Many times I have led people over the glacier,' he explained. 'I have even skied by myself over its entire length in one journey. But not in such weather as this. You do not know of the crevasse-fields to be crossed nor do you know the zigzag route we must follow if these dangerous areas are to be avoided. Also the Briksdalsbre itself – there are areas above it which will be perilous to cross and the ice-tongue itself I have never descended: indeed I know no one who has, for the cattle route has long since fallen into disuse.'

Jan Mickelbust was nodding his head vigorously and now interrupted.

'I know the weather in these parts – a mist like this may lie over the plateau for days on end and with it you will get the rain. Many of the snow-bridges will fall away and, as for the Briksdalsbre, all day and every day it will move with tons of falling ice. If you have any sense, you will abandon what equipment you cannot carry and descend to Fåberg.'

I noticed the others were standing around saying nothing, but contemplating the guides' words – meaningfully translated by Henrik.

The guides after all knew what lay ahead. We knew nothing – even our day's reconnaissance of the Briksdal glacier had been foiled by the necessity of a premature parachute jump. Perhaps the guides' words of wisdom were sinking-in to the little group as they waited shivering in the raw chill.

I returned to the attack.

'We cannot abandon the kit, Jan; the equipment on just one of those sledges costs more than 5,000 Krone. The Briksdal is steep and leads straight into a navigable stream. We may be able to lower all the kit on the sledges down the ice-face to the lake and have everything in the vehicles within three days. As you know this would not be possible by any of the other glacial tracks which are far more gradual and, anyway, end high up the valleys many miles short of a road or track. Even in a week we could not hope to get all this stuff down to Fåberg. You should have heard Henrik here complaining bitterly when he had to carry one heavy rucksack load down the Fåberg snout last week.'

Jan seemed to understand our dilemma and a sudden thought caused him to grasp David's arm. A rapid discussion followed between them. David at first shook his head but finally seemed to agree. He shrugged his broad shoulders with a weary grunt and then grinned at Henrik.

I could see then that he was keen to help us if he could: it was only his inborn sense of caution, the respect he held for these unpredictable mountains, that had prevented him from agreeing to our original requests. His face was rugged, full of character: he was a man on whom one could rely fully but who would never bite off more than he could chew.

Thinking that, I felt guilty since my own maxim – 'Where there's a will, there's a way' – was not the most realistic of outlooks.

Henrik now told us that the guides had reached a compromise. They would leave us at once and ski ahead some thirty kilometres to a point on the plateau where they would veer north to a rock route leading eventually down to Kvamme. At this point they would leave one of our axes in the ice pointing in the direction of the Briksdalsbre. We would have some ten kilometres to go after reaching the axe.

I asked Henrik what we should do if we lost the guides' spoor. He shrugged and indicated that further pressure on David would be useless.

It was settled. We shook hands with the Norwegians and parted amicably, watching for a while as they plodded off carrying their skis up the icy slopes to the plateau.

Then the toil began. For five hours we sweated, strained and cursed up the endless slopes. Each time we came to the top of a gradient, another expanse of grey mush-ice climbed to a misty horizon above us.

Bob, Henrik and I had a slightly lighter sledge than the others. Bob, the muscular rugby-player, was strapped to the traces, and doggedly tugged at the grudging load. Henrik and I trudged behind pushing as hard as we might, but irked by the rucksacks digging into our backs. Bob kept going doggedly in the clearly defined ski-spoor of the guides, stopping from time to time to check their direction with his compass bearing. His snow-goggles soon misted up with perspiration so he removed them. Strange how the snow should retain such a blinding glare when the mist obscured the faintest glimmer of the sun.

The drizzle had become light – almost unnoticeable. By midday, as we thankfully reached the edge of the plateau, we came above the mist so it seemed and into a sunny world of glistening ice-fields. Sparkling blue lines marked the split ice along the rim of the plateau and great was our relief on seeing the route ahead.

As far as the eye could see the shimmering white plateau rolled away to the west – flat as a pancake. If there were gradients they were undetectable.

Of the guides no sign; to our front we could see their spoor running on for little more than fifty yards before it faded into the overall glare. I began to wish I had snow-goggles, but they had been lost earlier that week.

We had a long wait for the others. Their load was decidedly the heavier and Geoff's ribs were paining him most of the time.

Mars bars and mouthfuls of snow recharged our batteries; then we clipped on the light skis and set off at a fine pace, the still-frozen surface hissing crisply as we glided smoothly west and the *půlk* soon gained sufficient momentum to run itself over the little 'moguls' which occurred with increasing frequency. These hard hummocks ran across the line of our route, formed by the violent wind and gouging rain. So long as we descended a faint incline they caused no bother, but later in the afternoon we began to climb again and were slowed to a snail's pace by the undulating snow-spoil.

No one talked; the earlier elation of leaving the mists was gone and we simply strained away at the traces thinking of nothing but the necessity of moving on without resting.

Then, as though to herald the Quatermas rising from its pit, curling billows of mist, layer upon layer, rose from the mountain flanks to our north and moved across our front.

Soon after moving into the first clammy tentacles of murk, we heard the rustling patter of light sleet on our anoraks. At that stage we had completed perhaps twenty kilometres and, since the guides' ski-trail had appeared very haphazard, conforming to no single bearing for any length of time, none of us had a definite idea of our whereabouts.

Now that the rains had begun again we must push on without delay though a rest would have been welcome. The snow had lost its crisp quality and, as the rain increased its sodden texture, the ski-spoor began – slowly but surely – to lose its clear outline. Where it passed over the smooth hummock tops, there was no visible mark and from time to time we had to stop to ascertain the direction of the trail, so indistinct and broken had it become.

Whenever the sledge stopped, its metal runners sank in and stuck to the ice-crust so that an extra effort was needed to tug it free. Henrik, stopped by a particularly abrupt 'mogul', had flung himself forward twice attempting to free the sledge runners, and drag the *pulk* over the obstacle.

Cursing with frustration, he jammed his ski-sticks into the ice and levered himself violently forwards. The leather harness snapped and Henrik's skis slipped backwards.

We mended the traces with thin nylon line but the repair took time, for our fingers were wet and numb with cold.

A wind howled about us lashing the sleet viciously into our eyes and lips.

We needed more grip with the skis to gain leverage for tugging our burdens but, as time passed and the crust grew wetter, the skis slid backwards more and more often. Just as one tried to pull hard to tug the *pulk* over a hummock, a ski would slip away backwards lashing into the sledge and causing one to fall.

Henrik bade us stop: he would re-wax our skis with a klister wax. Thankful for any excuse to rest our aching shoulders and thighs we sunk down in the poor shelter of the sledge. The others were not visible behind, but our own trail was plain to see since the whole floor area of our sledge was flattening the slush.

Henrik shook his head – running a gloved hand up one of his skis. Then he swore in some other tongue.

'Look at this. The abrasive texture of the surface-crust has ruined my skis. It will be no use at all trying to re-wax them and yours will be the same. New wax must always be applied on to a base wax, not direct to the wood, or it will rub off in minutes. But look – all the base wax has gone and much of the wood has been filed off too.'

We found our skis were similarly affected; the wood slightly splintered and in parts there was no wax at all. No wonder we were slipping about.

The others caught up with us. They too were slipping on the spot, 'tread-milling' as Roger described it, and they had stopped to repair their harness which had snapped on both sides.

Patrick looked pallid and cold, muttering about a tea-break. Bob heard him and began delving in a rucksack for tea-bags and hexamin fuel-cooker.

I grumbled that we couldn't afford to rest, for the guides' spoor was fading fast. Roger's face had also lit up at the mention of tea and I saw there was no hope of postponing this 'cha pause'. Furthermore if I complained too bitterly of delay, I might not get any of the tea-brew myself, so I shut up and crouched closer to the sledge.

But the wind was dashing across the ice-fields now and I was shivering uncontrallably long before the tea could boil. We drank the liquid tepid with more Mars bars and agreed to press on at once to keep some warmth in our bodies.

A gradually-descending slope helped us for two hours as we glided smoothly, silently, through the yellowish gloom, the driving sleet coming from behind us now, the cadence of its hiss on our anoraks rising and falling with the wind squalls.

We changed over the harnessed position every half-hour, the 'husky' making sure to look only before him, some five yards in front of his skis, to pick out the blurred marks of the faint piste.

Henrik touched me with his ski-stick and pointed to the left. We stemmed our skis and came to a grinding halt for there, like some long-sought signpost to Mecca, stood our ice-axe. Scrawled in the thin snow covering beside it were letters and an arrow. The letters were almost obliterated but Henrik, peering at them, shouted: 'TO BRIKSDALSBRE! . . . TO BRIKSDALSBRE!'

Then he came over and grasped my arm:

'Look, Ran, I must leave you here. I decided early this morning that it was better I leave once we reach this point. I did not want to leave with the Norwegians: you would not have managed with the packs and sledges with just five of you, but from here on must all be downwards. At the briefing in ice camp you told us that the descent would be entirely on a voluntary basis and none of us must feel forced to do it.'

'That's true Henrik, you must do what you want, but will you be all right by yourself? What if the guides' spoor fades out before you reach any trail cairns at the edge of the plateau?'

'I will be fine. Don't worry about me. I will leave you all the medical kit you might require and when I get down to the valley I'll let Johnnie know that you might not be above the Briksdal to-night since you have no guides and can see nothing in this foul weather. For God's sake take it carefully. I will make sure Johnnie keeps the radio open all the time in case you have troubles.'

The others arrived then, as relieved as we had been to find the ice-axe guide-mark.

None of them commented at the suggestion that the Kvamme trail was available for any who might care to take it.

Roger asked Henrik to stay on until we reached the upper reaches of the Briksdalbre, for no one liked the idea of his going off alone into the mist. But Henrik was determined. He was both experienced and highly capable and felt, probably quite rightly, that he would be of more use to us, in the event of an accident, if he were down below with a radio to correlate a rescue party if one became necessary.

We watched him ski off into the gloom and a faint feeling of loneliness, of the possible magnitude of the task which lay ahead, was enhanced by the wild moan of the wind shrilling through unseen rocks. Any of us could have chosen to leave by the Kvamme trail and would have felt justified in doing so; especially Bob and Patrick whose climbing experience was limited. All five, however, were keen to press on; anxious to find out what lay in store on the morrow. If there were risks involved, as each of us knew there might be, then each was taking his individual decision to face them.

Patrick set a compass-bearing carefully on our only map whilst Geoff held it down by the partial windbreak of a *půlk* – that map was gold-dust. Working on the assumption that we were virtually due north of the Kvamme ravine and knowing that the Briksdalsbre lay some nine kilometres along the edge of the plateau, Patrick's bearing was set to take us along the sloping rim and just above the level where we normally met crevasse-fields. He and Roger reckoned that a bearing of 4,400 mils moving at an average speed of three kilometres an hour would see us above the Briksdal ice-face in three hours without taking us too near the danger zones.

Bob moved out ahead of us with his compass: Geoff and I managing the *půlk* quite easily for the snow was smooth again and the ice hard. Patrick, between us and the rear sledge, shouted to Bob above the wind sound.

'Two degrees left! Go two degrees left!'

Bob's raucous yell floated back to us, 'What bloody use is that when my compass is scaled in mils!'

'Some architect you are, Powell, if you can't manage a simple conversion! Now go ten left, you're veering south much too much.'

Following Bob like a limpet, we moved carefully, finding that the gale was literally forcing the sledges to the left. Particles of icy sleet stung our cheeks and foreheads: the murky ether hissed with white pellets seemingly bent on our obstruction. Without goggles, I kept my eyes half-open and my head down, letting Geoff do the steering. I looked behind briefly from time to time: Patrick was there, swathed in mist, gliding silently as he checked Bob's direction on his own compass and shouting some new correction from time to time.

Of the other sledge there was no sign but they had our tracks to follow so long as they kept going. None of us wished to stop even briefly now; it was far too cold – the icy blast blowing straight up at us from the crevasse-fields down to our right. The booming explosion of falling ice came to us eerily, sometimes from quite close, and I expected at any moment to find the sloping shoulder which we traversed fall away sheer before us.

Bob must have had similar thoughts for he was moving more slowly now, peering myopically into the gloom and stemming his skis carefully.

I did not envy him his guiding role, for a crevasse can remain invisible in the mist until a skier is almost on top of it. It is difficult to stop quickly on langlauf skis when the surface is hard and icy.

We had been moving for two hours after leaving Henrik when Bob came to a sudden halt.

'Crevasse?' shouted Geoff.

'Yes, all over the place, we must have been moving with our eyes shut for they're on both sides.'

We had moved past some of the longest crevasses I had seen – quite without noticing them. The snow-bridges in this part of the glacier were firmer than those of the Fåbergstølsbre but they spanned wicked-looking gaps which ran on for hundreds of yards before tapering to some six feet in width. Only then did snow-bridges seal their lips where we could attempt to cross them; hearts thumping as the whole length of our sledge weighed down on a teetering span. We knew we should be roped but were too cold, too exhausted, to do aught but stumble on with heads down and shoulders bunched. Slithering skis catching in the crust, we shouted and cursed at each succeeding chasm which forced us from our compass bearing.

Wishing to go almost due west we spent most of the time trudging north and south searching for crossing points. Often two fissures would bottleneck into a cul-de-sac ending in a giddy 'lover's leap'. In such places, emerging from the mist, we would find ourselves on a perilously narrow peninsular, with no course open other than a cautious retreat to the far end of the seam in the hope of finding some way over. Geoff swore quietly, 'I'm glad we aren't crossing just there.'

Following his glance, I saw part of the white carpet to our left disappear in an unzipping action that ran along the ice for many yards – quite silently – leaving only the grinning black jaws of a crevasse.

It seemed unwise to spend a night in this unstable region but we must surely be somewhere above the Briksdalsbre. From all around came the booming echoes of falling ice. The crevasses had

The last four hundred feet of Briksdalsbre.

An ice traverse shortly before Patrick's accident.

confounded our sense of direction and it was no longer clear whether we should climb to the south or descend to the north in order to get out of the icy labyrinth.

A decision either way could lead us into deeper trouble.

I called to Bob to stop. We were traversing between two great splits, moving on an apparently solid platform as wide as a Roman Catholic altar is long. It offered no protection from the gale, but, on the Jostedal plateau, it is useless to look for shelter.

Unleashing the taut straps of the sledges with numb fingers was a slow business. With four of us gripping the corners of a tent, the fifth secured it, not with ice-pegs which were immediately whipped out by the wind, but with ice-axes pushed deep into the crust.

Inside, each of those tents was a pocket-paradise.

Roger too must have enjoyed the night's rest for his diary, normally impersonal, waxes warm:

> There is a sort of euphoria in the atmosphere inside a small tent pitched on a glacier. There is nothing, just nothing, like the comfort of a warm sleeping-bag, after a bad day on the Jostedal. The wind howls outside and the temperature drops well below zero; the tent flaps and billows making a most infernal din, but there is safety and warmth in a sleeping-bag, protected against the rude intrusion of the natural elements. One cannot compare the close companionship and humour between two friends huddled over a small gas-cooker, warming stew in a pot and thawing out numbed hands at the same time. The taste of brandy between cracked lips, a cigarette passed from mouth to mouth – all is well with the world . . .

Sufficient unto the day is the evil thereof, I mused, trying to sleep as strange rumblings, faint vibrations of the icy strife around us, kept at bay the growing muzziness of slumber.

Patrick's disembodied voice was calling monotonously.

'Hello Johnnie, this is Ice Party. Hello Johnnie, this is Ice Party.'

Perhaps Henrik had failed to find his way off the plateau, or else maybe the mist and gale was disrupting Patrick's transmission. I fell asleep to the rhythm of his plaintive litany.

I awoke briefly during the night thinking there were footfalls around the tent.

It was no nightmare, as I learnt next morning, for poor Bob's stomach had played him up and forced him out on to the ice to relieve himself.

'Definitely the coldest five minutes of my life,' said Bob, 'my arse nearly fell off. I tried Chris Bonington's Eiger method first but it didn't work as our tent door-holes are too small.'

I enquired what the Eiger climbers had done. According to Bob they had scooped ice for drinking water from the snow to the left of their tent doors, and defecated to the right.

Towards five o'clock next morning the mists cleared suddenly from below leaving us as though on the edge of a monsoon cloud. Immediately above us the mists still lay thick but elsewhere the world was a sun-dappled place beneath a clear friendly sky.

The events which followed were best witnessed by Bob Powell, for he moved behind the rest of us. His diary records the unfortunate incidents which might well have been crucial to our later survival:

> . . . 0545 hours. To our relief the clouds of mist rolled away and revealed a cold clear morning.
>
> We crawled from our tents and the whole of the top of the Briksdalsbre was unfolded. By back-bearings we established that we were in the position we had hoped for and we stowed the kit on the *půlks*, donned skis and set off for the upper icefield.
>
> Almost immediately disaster struck, for one of the *půlks* ran headlong out of control.
>
> Roger and Patrick fell sideways, releasing their grasp on the handles as the sledge crashed to oblivion into an ice-crack along with its valuable load. I attempted to halt its impetus but to no avail. We counted the cost of this loss – one boat, tents and parachutes, six hundred feet of rope and an assortment of personal and scientific gear, camp-beds, Lilos, etc.
>
> We continued down since, despite the loss, we still had all the necessities for the ice descent, but we did take the precaution of transferring loose items of personal kit such as the crampons and all the remaining ropes from the remaining sledge to our back packs.

Helmets were donned. We found a relatively simple route down the next steep gradient. Already though the crevasses were more formidable than those at the centre of the Fåbergstølsbre – some indication of what was to come.

No sooner had we congratulated ourselves on the speed with which we had navigated this first pitch – perhaps relaxing at the relative ease of the descent – when the second *půlk* went out of control.

So heavily laden were the two sledges that, traversing crabwise across the slope and having to turn through 180 degrees, was sufficient to throw them off balance and the second one rolled a bare three metres before plunging into a crevasse running parallel with our course. This time Patrick was on the downward side of the *půlk* and narrowly escaped being caught by the load as it rolled over. Roger was in the traces and was flicked bodily over. Ran and Geoff, navigating some two hundred metres ahead, turned but were in no position to help.

We grouped around the crevasse staring into the depths.

We had by now changed to crampons and one of the losses in this second incident was six pairs of skis and sticks strapped on the top of the *půlk* – indeed it was probably their bulk which had unbalanced the load and made it so ungainly.

We examined our kit laying it out on the snow to re-assess whether we had the bare minimum for the ice descent. Although much rope has been lost we decided that we should have sufficient lengths of 300-foot, 200-foot and 100-foot line, if single fixed ropes were used for abseils. Each team member had crampons and an ice axe and there was adequate food for twenty-four hours . . .

I winced as I thought of the amount of equipment lost. Perhaps it would have been better to have abandoned it above the Fåbergstølsbre and saved much sweat. On the other hand there had been a sporting chance of successfully lowering the sledges and a chance is always one up on a certainty.

There was little good to be had in worrying out that argument now however. At least we still had sufficient gear it appeared to descend three thousand feet of ice, however sheer, and all of us were fired with the desire to see what lay in store on the much vaunted Briksdalsbre.

Patrick tried further radio contact with Johnnie but there was no reply. We edged our way warily down the fissured gradient coming safely to the black horn of granite that descends sheer to the western flank of the great ice-tongue. From here we had our first glimpse of Norway's most notorious glacier.

EIGHT

Between the Ice Falls

BENEATH US LAY A vast field of jagged ice-blocks; a nightmare in blue and white; an inferno of brilliant reflected and refracted light piercing the eye and mind so that for a long while we lay silent, contemplating the forces which caused so chaotic a scene. The more startling to us after the mind-numbing neutrals of grey mist and snow rendered opaque by the driving blizzard of the preceding days.

This was the first ice-fall. There would be four more but only this one could safely be skirted by descending the black cliffs enclosing its either edge, for here the rock was broken in many places and the route beside the ice-fall would be an uncomplicated rock descent saving valuable hours of light. Time was all-important for, with our remaining rations and all but a single two-man tent lost in the crevasse-field, we could ill afford to spend another night on the ice.

The lake which lay at the base of the glacier was not to be seen, being hidden by the bulging ice-arm which we must descend. The deep green of the Briksdal valley was hazy and infinitely far below our little party. A white flicker, a flashing sliver of light slitting the gloom of the still shadowed valley, indicated the course of the cataract of glacial water running fast through unseen ravines to Oldenfjord.

Patrick and Bob had not climbed on ice or rock before – apart from our days working on the Fåbergstølsbre – and since their rucksacks weighed sixty pounds apiece with the additional bulk of the heavy Marlow ropes, any tricky stretch requiring delicate balance meant removing their packs and lowering them separately; this was ponderous and it was noon by the time we reached the base of the slippery rock.

A waterfall precluded further movement between ice and rock; a thunderous deluge issuing from the heavens so it seemed, for the water's source was invisible to us huddled down below. Flashing cascades poured forth from the black granite many hundreds of feet above us, thundering past ice and rock into some bottomless canyon. From this subterranean maelstrom strange sounds as of the damned came floating up causing my head to swim with vertiginous stirrings. Thoughts of Poe's remoter nightmares chilled my mind . . . and Coleridge's 'caverns measureless to man through down to a sunless sea'.

Such a watery obstacle was not to be passed: we should have to cross on to the ice and leave the rock-face from now on. But this would not be simple for a formidable gap, known as the *bergschrund*, nearly always separates the side-walls of a flowing ice-arm from the rock of its enclosing valley cliffs. Fast-running water, black alluvial slime and subterranean landslides of rock and ice make a *bergschrund* an inhospitable region for climbers.

Looking carefully around we saw that instead of the usual giddy divide between rock and glacier we were faced, through some anomaly of nature's forces, with a temporary bridge of ice spanning the abyss. It looked as if a great chunk of ice had lodged itself in the *bergschrund* when the last avalanche had descended from the towering ice-face above. Other smaller bits of ice had then wedged upon the original chunk so that although the latter giant had melted down and might at any moment drop away into the gorge, a complex of crazily balanced blocks led the way before our doubtful gaze on to the main ice-arm.

Roger was with me and viewed the teetering bridge with equal distaste.

'Any further movement from above which hits this will remove it completely, you know.'

I nodded. 'I couldn't agree more but we can't go back and there's no other way down. The sun's at its zenith and once on to the ice we'll have to move fast to the centre of the arm or risk these falls. The whole thing looks dicey, but we must move across now or we'll be stuck in the middle of that lot tonight when the ice starts contracting and the whole place is alive with falling chunks.'

It was good to have Roger up front with me for, older and more cautious, he hated rushing things. This annoyed me, but that was my fault. He kept quoting some Italian saying which roughly added up to 'more haste – less speed'. In view of the snail-like pace at which the others were descending, this niggled me. However, his way was the right way; I realised this – subconsciously at any rate; he had been on countless expeditions and watched people die through carelessness. Maybe he was cursing me for bringing him to this unsavoury spot where the dangers were objective and unavoidable, for nothing we did, no precautions we took, could guarantee our safety. Any chance fall would sweep away the five little orange flies from this almost human *bre*. Maybe they were all cursing me as they slithered down the wet scarred rock and felt the raw power of the elements take charge of them in a way they had never experienced before.

I contemplated the ice-bridge, as we clung to the rock awaiting the others, averting my gaze from the drop below; trying to ignore the sounds of turmoil and the first booming shock waves of ice-falls above and below. I knew why I felt irritated; I was frightened and the roots of my hair exuded a clammy sweat which I could feel and despised. I glanced at Roger, but he seemed unaffected by his surroundings. Perhaps he guessed my feelings. Did he feel that he should be leading us? After all, I had never climbed on ice before any more than the others. Our week's clambering about the Fåbergstølsbre was the only experience any of us could boast. A few days ago we had strapped on crampons – probably incorrectly since no one knew how the experts wore them – and, grasping the alien weight of short ice-axes, taken our first uncertain steps on the treacherous medium of glacial ice. But the Fåbergstølsbre was a gentle slope compared with this monster; both in length and degree of incline.

This was no time for lack of self-confidence; ice is not so very dissimilar to rock when it comes to methods of descent and I had spent much of my life in various mountain ranges. The others had not; so I was, I tried to persuade myself, the best qualified to pioneer a route down the Briksdalsbre. My temporary and unreasonable irritation with Roger soon subsided but it brought back to me memories of another occasion when I had allayed strong feelings, though then they had been of misery not fear.

* * *

Coming to England at eleven years of age, I had been sent to a private school in Wiltshire. South African education had set me back a couple of years behind my age group and an Afrikaans twang to my accent was quickly pounced on by the school bullies. One particular fellow made my life miserable although I was slightly his senior. He was a ratty freckled-faced boy who – many years later – made off with my current girl friend and married her.

One summer term I found that my tormentor had been allotted to the small attic dormitory of which I was nominally in control. He flouted my theoretical authority at every opportunity and my helpless hatred of him grew. On a balmy night in August, the school fire-alarm was sounded. The boys in each dormitory grabbed their dressing-gowns, jammed on slippers and lined up by their windows. Each dormitory captain rushed to his respective window to attach the waiting winch and harness to its hook. It was his oft practised duty to lower each boy to the ground below, having first strapped them to the harness at the end of the winch-rope. He, like the skipper of a ship, would go last.

It had not in fact been one of the many methods I had contemplated of disposing of my *bête noire*. He had been boiled wriggling in bubbling oil; he had screamed his lungs out in hot deserts whilst strapped to ant-hills, he had often had his limbs sawn off slowly to the tune of a current Elvis Presley melody, but never had so elementary and satisfactory an answer suggested itself to me in the many classroom hours wasted away in plans of morbid revenge. He held on to the thin cord and, all unsuspecting, closed his eyes to avoid seeing the seventy-odd feet which separated him from the ground where a matron and the other boys waited in the dark. I pulled the harness around him and went through the motions of clipping it up, failing only to close the vital retaining clasp. I had but to order him out now . . . a short sharp free-fall and summary execution for his juvenile nastiness. But being Piscean and not violent of nature, I crushed this inner sparkle of malevolence and completed the safety couplings to watch the brute descend under control: reluctant reprieve for this embryonic Sadist.

* * *

Some forty minutes after Roger and I had arrived at the *bergschrund*, Geoff appeared beside us bleak-eyed and obviously perturbed. The other two, still out of sight above us, were making heavy going judging by the veritable shower of pebbles and bits of scree that clattered off our helmets and rucksacks as we ducked. Geoff was blunt-spoken.

'They're both climbing like pregnant frogs; using their knees and elbows and, probably because of the heavy packs, their balance is non-existent. I've tried getting them to lower the packs separately but it takes far too long and dislodges rocks.'

The sun was homing west; we must go faster but there was so much equipment weighing us down. Patrick arrived and, like a punctured Lilo, sunk down by us; not speaking.

Bob slithered after him kicking gravel-spray away into the void.

'Let's have a short rest. I'm knackered and my pack's a bastard.'

So we sat together and the alarming nature of the vista was very evident.

'Fantastic!' said Patrick without enthusiasm. 'What in God's name am I doing here on this bloody ice-block. I'm sure to be killed before we get anywhere near the bottom of this thing. My rucksack's killing me and I'm exhausted. The whole thing's crazy. It might be all right for you lot as you're fit but I've been sitting in an office for months.'

There didn't seem anything appropriate to say. Morale appeared to be waning as quickly as the sun.

I strapped on crampons and took the ice-axe from my pack. There were three hundred feet of thin red rope coiled loop on loop and strapped to the top of the pack. Specially-designed 8-plat matt Terylene which weighed less per foot than our personal hempen ropes but these were only a hundred feet in length. I began to uncoil my red rope.

Each of the others carried similar ropes of different colours and Roger had carefully strapped to his Bergen the sturdy Racal radio – our only contact with the road party who should by now be at the lake below. There would be no way for them to drive the vehicles up the steep valley, so they were to trek up from the tourist restaurant below the lake, bringing with them rations and the two Avon boats. They would make a temporary camp by the side of the lake from where they could check our descent through binoculars and advise us by radio as to the best route down.

As the others readjusted their packs and tightened crampons, Roger tuned the radio minutely and tried to contact the camp far below.

Johnnie Muir answered him; his voice sounding far away but relief very evident in his tone. He had bad news; news which he had learnt from some locals earlier that morning and which he had been trying to tell us about ever since; keeping his radio open permanently and sending another set higher up the valley with Peter Booth and a guide to man it. Now, hearing us at last, Johnnie was voluble. He couldn't understand why we had not been told before – since it was common knowledge amongst the local Norwegians – that the glacier we were descending was notoriously dangerous throughout the year owing to its unusually steep declivity, but during mid-August, the period of maximum annual melting activity, it was especially hazardous. Some forty local farmers and guides had walked up to the lake and sat with Johnnie and the girls discussing our plight – for such they unanimously considered it to be. Fifty years ago they said, a Briton called William Slingsby, a climber of much repute, had managed to scale the *bre*; but his attempts at descending it had been frustrated by the falling ice and the impossibility of working out a plausible return route. Whereas he had planned his upward route carefully in advance, he could not retrace it once up, for such is the nature of the ice that crevasses may be jumped across in one direction but often not the other. Going up, he could see to avoid the more perilous pitches; not so descending – for the ground below was dead ground visually.

For half a century the great face had remained inviolate and then, only five days before our own arrival at its summit, a team of Norway's ace glacier climbers had set out at dawn and, after forty gruelling hours – and an accident when the leader had badly strained his ankle – they had been forced to give up only a thousand feet from the top. Later they were to describe the ascent as their most difficult climb ever. Their achievement was the culmination of months of training and numerous ascents of other tamer glaciers. They acknowledged the Briksdalsbre to be the Everest of Norway's *bres*. They had been equipped with the latest in ice-climbing gear, specially stressed screws and pitons, and periscopic ice-ladders for traversing the many wide crevasses, which split the entire breadth of the *bre* in places.

'Had this team come down again?' asked Roger. There was a pause whilst Johnnie consulted an English-speaking Norwegian, then his reply.

'Definitely not, the dangers of descent on such faces are more unpredictable than a pre-planned, pre-routed climb according to the local know-alls. They say you should go back while you can.'

Roger repeated this to us but none of us commented.

'We cannot go back, Johnnie. Both sledges and most of the survival kit were lost this morning. We're virtually out of food with no spare radio batteries and only one two-man tent between the five of us. Getting this far has meant traversing a maze of crevasse-fields and a long descent. It's unlikely we would ever find a way back even if the weather remains fine.'

I took the head-sets from Roger and asked Johnnie if the locals thought a helicopter could remove us from our predicament. Again a pause and then an uncompromising reply.

'There are already two helicopters on standby within an hour's journey but Jan Mickelbust here says they could never do it. For one thing the thermal wind-currents up the glacial valley would make it impossible to hover above you and between the narrowly separated cliffs. For another, the helicopter's engine noise and the downward blast from its blades would set off many avalanches and bury the lot of you. You don't seem to understand that you've chosen the very worst time of year for this. Everything's melting. From down here its like listening to Tchaikovsky's *1812*. Each new explosion is followed by a minute spume of white spray. Looking at these through binoculars we can see whole areas of the face break off and fall away; chunks of ice bounding down the glacier below. If you really can't go back, for heaven's sake be careful and take your time. I'll keep the radio open, so let me know if you get in difficulties. We can't actually see you as yet, so I can't tell you much about the conditions below you.'

Roger closed down the radio, so with Geoff well belayed to a boulder by my red rope, I stepped gingerly on to the ice, and was immediately conscious of its unstable quality, for – rather like wet shingle on a sloping beach – the top layer of ice was made up of blue melting cubes slipping slowly downwards of their own volition as one watched, so that a perpetual dribble of them slid into space from that precarious gangway. Prodding for a firmer base beneath this shale, I dug a crampon into a solid block some two-foot by three-foot. It shuddered but held, so I edged slowly and evenly across to the largest block, digging axe and one crampon in firmly on the more stable chunks before taking another step across. Resting by a central ice-pillar it was painfully clear how temporary was the nature of this ice-bridge, for here the main wedged block had melted to its narrowest and only a few minor pieces had settled on it; none very satifactorily. Between them I could see down into the *bergschrund* below whence came the noise of rushing water and subterranean ice-falls crashing against rock gullies as they slid away. I looked back and saw Geoff paying out my rope slowly from the shoulder; as he waited patiently for me to reach the stable ice ahead where I in turn would secure myself and belay him over the bridge. Geoff is a solid man, I thought, the type one can rely on. He makes no noise, no fuss, but in his quiet way he knows all the answers. I was planning an eighteen month's Arctic journey for two years hence but had no thoughts for a suitable companion. It crossed my mind at that moment that the enigmatic Geoff would be the ideal sledging mate for two hard years in the icy ulu.

I trod warily on two of the balanced blocks but both pivoted wildly and I withdrew my questing boot rapidly as from a too-hot bath. There seemed no way over this crumbling ledge. Geoff whistled with low cadence and indicated the far side of the ice-pillar. Slithering round it I found a narrow but firm block wedged at its base and eased around the bottleneck with caution, for the weight of the pack tended to pull my body outwards. I noticed the pillar was red where I had clutched it. My woollen army gloves must have succumbed to the abrasion of sharp rock and ice and now my epidermis was also being torn by the file-like surface of the eroded blocks. Ten minutes of intricate movement and I was across the bridge and, cutting holds up the face of the solid ice, climbed on to a narrow ridge where it was possible to belay to a home-made ice-bollard. 'Thank God we will never see that bottomless *bergschrund* again,' I muttered to Geoff as he clambered up to the ridge.

'Don't start counting any chickens yet,' he whispered, 'there's almost certainly worse to come.'

The others crossed without incident, but Bob had snapped off the rear section of one crampon. This was bad since we had another two thousand feet to descend on sheer wet ice and crampons were decidedly the most vital item of all the equipment. Our spare pairs had been on the *půlk* sledges and so were now in cold preservation. We took a rope from Bob to lighten his load and improve his balance, but the hours ahead would be no joke for him.

Once on to the ice we made faster progress. A maze of tumbled blocks led down to an almost flat plateau as wide as a football field: the far end of which ended abruptly – presumably with a major precipice. Ice-axes flashed, digging ledges for the crampon spikes, and one by one we descended to the plateau by a tortuous route through, around, even under, the labyrinth of blue pinnacles. Bob recorded our arrival at the plateau in his diary:

> The ice fall negotiated, we traverse across to what looks to be the quicker central route. Ran has, by the time I reach the centre, already fixed a double 200-foot abseil rope and one by one we lower ourselves to the plateau above the final 2,000-foot pitch. The plateau itself is some 400 yards wide and crossing this is no mean feat in itself. It is difficult to recapture the sheer hard work and time it takes to perform even a simple manoeuvre. The negotiation of the ice-fall for example – all carried out with whispered commands, for even a whistle can bring a ton of ice crashing down – took about one and a half hours.

Rushing rivulets flowed down every cranny in the ice and thirsty with apprehension and fatigue, we lay on the ice to lap up the nectar-like water and bathe bloody hands. It had not been apparent from above but the plateau was split by a series of parallel fissures. It resembled a ploughed field – only each furrow was many feet in depth and from three to six feet wide at the lips. We began to zigzag through this crevasse-field wishing we had but a single ice-ladder – or even a sledge – to bridge these alarming gaps. To begin with the fissures would narrow towards either flank and by side tracking to left or right we could find places where it was possible to jump across the gaps: cramponned feet scrabbling for a hold on landing. But, not half-way across the plateau, we came to a great crack that stretched across the whole breadth of the glacier. No one would volunteer to jump across with a rope – all were apparently still sane.

We would have to back-track – horrible thought – and detour round the obstacle by finding a way over the *bergschrund* and down the cliff-face. This was easier said than done, for although on the western flank the ice flowed very close to the rock, the latter was smooth as glass. Roger spotted a plausible route down an ice gully. Looking down it, he had spotted a ledge running almost horizontally across the rock and sloping gently downwards. We could abseil down to this and continue our descent within the dark *bergschrund* and beneath the dripping wall of the frozen glacial river.

Looking back to the plateau I saw one orange figure lying crumpled on the ice, well behind us.

'It's Patrick,' said Roger, 'he's whacked and resting.'

Evening was nigh with the five of us in the middle of an ice-wall which at any moment might prove impossible to descend. Already a cold wind was blowing up the gully and even a five-minute halt had us shivering uncontrollably. We would need sustenance and warm shelter but had neither. This was no time to rest and my temper flared. I swore at Patrick, yelling at him to join us at once. This had no effect on him but the echoes of my voice melded with the booms of responsive ice-falls above and below adding weight to my urgency. He got up, teetering as the pack settled on his shoulders, and plodded up to join us in a daze.

Roger, Bob and Geoff descended into the gloom and I lowered

their packs on a separate rope. Patrick next. I prodded him and he shook his head as though awakening. He looked around following the snaking red line of his rope. Then he shouted in alarm.

'Where's Geoff? Good God, he's gone down a crevasse! Come quickly. Help me with the rope; we must pull him out!'

Patrick, accustomed to seeing Geoff on the other end of his rope, had not seen him detach himself and descend into the *bergschrund*. Geoff's end of the rope had snaked away into a crevasse and Patrick, to his horror, had drawn the obvious conclusion. I reassured him that Geoff was still in the land of the living and soon the five of us were edging our way along a dripping rock-ledge deep within the gloomy *bergschrund*. The resonant gurgle of streams sucked through channels of alluvial mud and icy shale came up to us; and our whispered remarks came sighing back as in an echo chamber.

'This place is bad for our morale,' joked Geoff, 'the sooner we get back into daylight the better.'

The ledge might have been wider, and water dripped down the backs of our necks, but at least it went in the right direction. We had followed it for three hundred yards and assumed we must have circumvented the great fissure which had blocked our way on the surface above. The ledge kept its level of incline, but the ice-arm began to descend rapidly and soon its upper lip was again horizontal with us but some six yards away from our little ledge. It was dusk, I realised with some surprise, and a freezing wind blew steadily up the Briksdalsbre. Even if we could get back on to the ice, it would be unwise to do so in the poor light. We agreed to spend the night on the ledge – there being no reasonable alternative.

There was a single tent designed to sleep two average-sized soldiers in comfort, so long as they have Lilos or soft ground beneath them. We brushed the wet gravel from our miniscule camping ground, erected the tent and crawled inside through the small entrance-flap. What a squeeze. It was too cold outside to do aught but take spare clothes from our rucksacks and leave the latter wedged against the rock with vital ropes and axes where no freak gale might remove them. The maddening business of removing boots from swollen feet with numb fingers was conducted inside the tent – one man at a time – whilst the others laughed at his ineptitude. Blood began to return to our toes and fingers so that they ached intolerably. There was nothing to clean them with – for no one was willing to leave the shelter of the tent for water – but Patrick produced some evil-looking yellow cream from his anorak and this we applied to the raw areas of our fingers, for he swore it was antiseptic. The writing on the tube was in Latin and Bob accused him of having it for a very different reason. Whatever its true purpose, its effects were agonising and my fingers kept me awake much of the night. Patrick, Bob and Geoff had tough civilian gloves and their fingers were but slightly cut. Roger, like me, had army woollen mitts, so his hands were raw and swollen.

'Good heavens,' said Patrick with unusual animation, 'it's my birthday today!'

Even the medicinal brandy was finished and Roger's search for the methylated spirits proved fruitless. But a tattered pack of playing cards was found and a poker school commenced at which Patrick lost more Norwegian Kroner than the rest of us. He was allowed an extra desertspoonful of the mashed curry gruel which Roger prepared in the centre of the tent: this meant two spoonfuls instead of one, three sips of weak tea instead of two – for we were each rationed to a fifth of one man's 'dehydrated meal'. I had visions of all those ration packs which, that very morning, had cart-wheeled into a crevasse on the runaway sledges. We sat in a huddled circle smoking wet cigarettes with relish. Geoff, our resident Sapper and explosives expert, regaled us with war-time stories of the incredible sophistication with which booby traps were laid.

'There was this Guards' officer and his platoon. He'd been in action for five months and knew all the tricks, or thought he did. The Germans were withdrawing faster than before but they would often booby-trap anything worth looting. The platoon arrived by night in this little village and, finding Jerry had gone, they planned to rest for a couple of hours before advancing farther. The young lieutenant was soon snoring in a barn but his sergeant woke him. "Hey, sir, take a load of this: she's blonde, beautiful and alone in bed." The officer leapt from his hay – his boots were already on and his pistol holstered on his belt, for, as I say, he knew it all – and followed his sergeant down the street to a little cottage. A light was on in the front room and peeping

Geoff leading the
second rope.

Roger freezes as a subterranean avalanche passes beneath his feet.

Negotiating the broken ice of the Briksdalsbre.

through the curtains at his sergeant's signal, he saw this voluptuous fräulein reading in bed. The sergeant grinned in anticipation. "We'll have to interrogate her, won't we, sir?" But the young officer knew better than to rush in, for he knew all the tricks Jerry could ever devise. "Fetch some rope, Sergeant." The rope having duly arrived, the subaltern tied one end to the fräulein's door and, seeing a convenient trench twenty yards away, knelt down in it with the Sergeant holding the end of the rope.

' "Now pull, Sergeant, and you'll never trust Jerry again!"

'The sergeant tugged hard, the door clicked open, and the trench blew up.'

Our laughter died away and we listened to the thump and boom of a nearby fall.

'Enough to drive a bloke barmy,' Bob mused.

We knew that tomorrow would be sheer precipice for two thousand feet – the famous moving ice-arm which tourists from all over the world come to see and record for their home movies the drama and the beauty of falling ice.

We decided that we would sleep like sardines – one up, one down and head to toe. This made for more room, true enough, but our hips were jammed solid in the middle of the tent. Furthermore, with due respect to Patrick and Geoff, between whom I was wedged, so overpowering was the aroma from their four feet, that I was soon nodding off despite the nearby crunch and rumble of the ice.

NINE

Avalanche!

After two hours in the 'black hole of Calcutta', I awoke with someone's bony hip jabbing my rib-cage to find the aroma was nauseous as well as soporific. Even the freezing wind outside might be an improvement, but how to extricate myself from the tightly packed bodies without waking them? Being a captive in my sleeping-bag it was impossible and foul mutterings from unidentifiable mouths followed me as I retreated through the tiny entrance-hole.

Another night of equal discomfort sprang to mind as I shivered on the ledge outside the tent in the icy wind. Some years earlier I had been on what is officially described as 'continuation training' with the 22nd Special Air Service Regiment.

In groups of four we had spent many days in the Welsh hills evading detection and arrest by the various regiments whose sole task it was to find us. Our daily rations were live broiler chickens left at obscure and usually distant grid references in the hills. Instructions would also be left in this manner and on the evening in question we found orders to lay our dummy charges at midnight within the Transfynydd power station. This was many miles away and, after a long walk, we found ourselves three miles from our goal with only half an hour in hand. One of the group, a little Scots paratrooper, noticed on his map that a railway curved up the mountainside towards our destination. Whilst following it we found a four-wheeled rail trolly with a centrally pivoted cranking handle. With the four of us moving the crank energetically back and forth, the trailer moved at a respectable speed up the gradient. Some four hundred yards from the top we came to a sudden halt and soon found that a large chock-lever blocked our advance. Picking the trailer up bodily, we put it back on the rails on the far side of the chock and carried on to the terminal buffers close by the power station.

We completed our task and retired by a different route.

Not much later, another group of 'saboteurs', having also laid their charges, and keen to leave the area quickly – as dawn was breaking – found the trolly and set off downhill at a very fine pace.

Soon the crank was moving back and forth like a piston and the trolley going like the wind to the delight of its passengers. Their joy was short-lived, as we later heard, for they hit the chock-lever at speed, the trolley halted abruptly and they, still clutching their rifles, went into orbit.

The same night my group was captured by a large body of Irish Fusiliers who detained us with another captive group in a derelict house. To ensure our security we were partially stripped and handcuffed in a long line. Since we were wet through from rain, and that February was unusually cold, it was necessary to lie in a closely huddled bundle on the floor to keep at all warm. Every time one of the eight wished to urinate, the whole line would be woken and would shuffle shivering to the far wall where a basin lay; the unfortunate culprit usually finding, on reaching the basin to the curses of his fellows, that he 'couldn't' after all.

Much was my embarrassment, and of a similar nature, when I found the ledge on the Briksdalsbre intensely cold and decided that the evil atmosphere of the tent could only be an improvement.

During my brief absence from the tent the other four had fallen asleep again and seemed to have swollen. I tried to drive a foot between two of the bodies as a thin edge of the wedge but there was no room in the inn, and I spent the night outside regretting my lack of staying power.

Dawn came cold and clammy creeping up the deep blue of

the ice: a heavy curtain slowly rising to reveal a stage set for some strange drama.

Breakfast was three-quarters of a biscuit; exactly three-quarters, for I checked carefully – lest there had been a mistake and I was due the whole. A tin mug full of steaming water well boiled with used tea-bags was passed around under Bob's stern eye. Should a drinker's Adam's apple jerk more than once, or the tilt of the mug be too acute, Bob's large hand would strike and the mug be passed to the next man.

Visions of scrambled egg and fruit juice – not iced.

Hands ached and refused to operate efficiently with bootlaces, zips and rope coils. Blisters squelched and complained bitterly at the first pressure of bootleather, but, to the general disappointment, Bob's lips no longer had their morning bleed – for Boots' lip-salve was working wonders where Henrik's Finnish and Polish potions had wrought havoc.

Geoff's ribs were as tender as ever but he was up first and, lying along the ledge to peer downwards, pondered our next step.

He decided on a long abseil down the sheer wet rock to a narrow guttering nearly three hundred feet below which protruded from the cliff so that it lay over and above the ice, bridging the *bergschrund* neatly though precariously.

There was a 300-foot length of Marlow Multiplait coiled around Bob's rucksack which Geoff used, securing it by a sling and carabiner to a hefty boulder on the ledge.

The descent was unnerving and served to jolt us wide awake, stretching stiff limbs and bringing feeling to our hands.

To prevent rope-burn, my tattered gloves being worse than useless, I wrapped socks around my hands. These were soaked in blood on my breathless arrival at the guttering below but, for the first time since the previous morning, my hands felt warm and the throbbing had ceased.

Patrick was unusually quiet, although his progress was as noisy as ever, loose rocks and gravel particles showering down on those of us below as he jerkily descended the rope. He must be a brave man, I thought, for he had a strong dislike for heights and that first abseil was of a decidedly exposed nature.

To miss the guttering meant to dangle over the wide gaping jaws of the fissures beneath: the rope had reached the guttering with perhaps fifteen feet to spare. Geoff's estimation had been precise but the view from above was misleading, for, although our narrow guttering effectively bridged the *bergschrund*, it was higher above the ice than we had thought. To jump on to the ice would be suicidal, even with crampons, since the surface was hopelessly fractured – being the jagged spoil of many previous ice-falls lying poised in unstable confusion over the deep canyons.

The sun was not yet over the mountains and the narrow ledge where we clung to the wet granite was a dank chilly place.

The ice below looked to my inexperienced eyes totally impossible; a hostile area of innumerable death-traps, where one step on an ill-balanced ice-block would cause a whole delicately poised platform to collapse into the void below. A noise, too, might be enough to set in motion the tumbled fragments from above, and bring them bounding through the air to sweep the face and fall to the unseen lake a thousand feet below.

I shuddered involuntarily and looked upwards over my shoulder. The rope swayed gently, running out of sight up the slimy cliff. We could not get it down – a fact which delighted Bob whose load was that much lighter.

We would not get back that way, I mused, so we had no choice but to descend – having burnt our boats thoroughly.

It was getting cold standing tight against the rock and staring at the frozen waterfall of ice so near to us, yet so unattainable. Again Geoff's keen and practical eyes found us a way out. There was, he said, a series of sharp runnels in the rock running diagonally across the cliff to our left as we faced the ice. If we could make our way down by way of them we would reach a point where a large tumble of ice had jammed over the *bergschrund*; this Geoff felt sure was our only way out, up or down.

Patrick, following behind in his usual unsteady fashion, lurched up to the obstacle and verbally indicated his reluctance to follow such a precarious route.

'You must be joking,' he muttered, inspecting the route indicated by Geoff. 'A monkey with sticky fingers would look twice at that.'

I must have spoken angrily to Patrick then for I sparked off a violent soliloquy which indicated very clearly what he thought of the whole proceedings. I was accused of being totally unaware of the perils of the situation, of abusing his friendship by deceitfully luring him on to the expedition with false promises of trout-fishing in Norwegian Lakes, ski-ing in the hot northern sun, and little physical discomfort apart from the odd night in a tent. Indeed, he had been led to believe that there was every likelihood of his being able to live in the manner and style to which he was accustomed.

Once this indignant tirade had abated, Patrick obviously felt better and crabbed his way past us to inspect the slimy rock-face.

As Geoff reiterated, there really wasn't anywhere else to go, and, ten minutes later, Patrick was following Bob on a delicate traverse round the series of smooth bluffs which led gradually down to the ice-fall.

Only the sharply eroded runnels in the granite provided holds. Some were too smooth to grip, but, with a fist clenched within them, good chock-holds served to keep us from falling away from the bluffs.

We clung like limpets to each little hold, cursing the outward pull of the rucksacks and sweating at the thought of what lay below. But we made it and reached a hollow in the rock on a level with the giant blocks of the ice-fall.

Here we strapped on crampons and loosed the ice-axes from our packs.

Geoff would move behind Bob and Patrick on a single 200-foot Terylene rope, Roger and I keeping slightly ahead but taking care not to move below them at any stage.

And so began the most hair-raising morning of my life. The upper cliffs of the Briksdalsbre are at no stage predictable but at least their dangers can be minimised by care and common sense. That is no longer true when one comes to the bottle-neck region which crests the final majestic sweep to the lake, a sheer thousand feet of brittle ice swept by avalanches throughout the summer months.

From the first few testing steps over the ice-fall it was obvious that only luck would see us safely down the next teetering gradient.

There was no longer the feeling of exposure as experienced on the rock, for here we were tacking across the face moving sideways as much as downwards and often dwarfed by needle-sharp pinnacles protruding from the face.

There were layers of brash ice; loose particles no bigger than footballs strewn amongst larger jagged blocks that balanced haphazardly one upon the other.

I halted abruptly as a grinding rush of smaller fragments slid away before my eyes to disappear as though down a trapdoor. Where they had been, a deep blue cavern lay revealed and the rectangular block on which I crouched lurched sickeningly, slipping towards the newly opened hole with other bigger blocks moving beside it. I wanted to scream or shout or something, but stopped instinctively.

Another block, sliding down before mine moved across the gap and plugged it.

I breathed again and prayed hard with meaning. Roger had seen my predicament but had wisely stayed where he was. Fascinated I watched as he too crossed the thin platform and joined me on a hard ridge on the far side.

For minutes we surveyed the chaotic scene below. Layer upon layer of fallen blocks were scattered crazily between tall chiselled pillars. The blue sheen of raw ice was covered by black slime, for the alluvial muck of the *bergschrund* higher up had spewed these fragments through diagonally inclined fissures and down to the ice-cliffs below.

A thunderous roar sounded above us – coming immediately after a report much like a pistol crack. I ducked instinctively – wondering if the entire face would be covered by what was to come.

The shoulder on which we kneeled seemed to shudder and vibrate as the whole ravine reverberated with appalling sound density. A squadron of Concordes passing directly above might have produced a similar volume of sound, but I doubt it. All around us the smaller ice-fragments slid away as the first great chunk bounded past, well to our front. Then the main body of pounding, gyrating white boulders passed with alarming speed, flaying the smaller pinnacles and sending slivers of glinting ice all about us.

The pulsating roar passed away, echoes and re-echoes pursuing the mother sound down the enclosing cliffs of the gorge till silence came and we looked at one another, saying nothing.

We were descending slowly, very slowly. It was already ten o'clock, and the sun would soon climb over the mountains. Then we would be in trouble for the melting process would accelerate ice-falls.

Already the little mountain track far below was moving with pinpricks of colour; the first tourists from Loen trekking up from the road head to watch and photograph the fabulous ice-falls of the Briksdalsbre.

The thought was ironic. Here we were dreading the next fall, praying that the sun delay its climb – whilst down below, on the far side of the lake, the tourists gaped up impatient for an avalanche, the bigger the better, and wishing the sun were up. They could not know that five fellow-humans were moving snail-like down the wall of death.

A sudden cry of fear shrilled over the ice and I stopped. Roger was belaying me across a slippery ledge traversing above a patch of loose shale. The others were fifty yards behind and visible.

Geoff was moving far too quickly. He had laid down his rucksack and was jumping recklessly from block to block. Then I saw why. Patrick, in the middle of the rope, had disappeared through a heap of loose shale. He must have trodden on the slippery stuff and been swallowed up as it gave way. He would have fallen into the waiting chasm but Bob, hearing his cry, had dropped between two large ice-boulders and arrested the snaking rope. Now Patrick dangled somewhere below the surface.

Roger and I were prevented from turning round, so narrow and precarious was our ledge: we could only watch and hope.

As Geoff reached the area of the slide he slipped and further fragments fell in on top of Patrick, one large block closing over the hole to form a tomb.

I wanted to shout at Geoff, to warn him to secure himself first – but any noise was a danger – and he began to heave clear the chunks above Patrick. He was attached only to Patrick's rope, which was small comfort, and my heart was in my mouth as I watched him working madly at the ice. Bob strained at the rope lying flush in his well-chosen nook.

Fortune was with us; the ice held and balancing his outstretched legs between slanting chunks, Geoff began to haul on the rope with Bob's aid. Patrick surfaced a few minutes later, numb with cold but unhurt. There was no time to rest, so we continued once Geoff had lightened Patrick's rucksack.

It took us two hours to descend the cracked expanse; poor Bob slithering on his broken crampon but always saving himself through his natural strength and sense of balance. Patrick continued to slip and fall for he was mentally and physically exhausted and his unfit leg muscles were unwilling to stand the strain of the pack and the strenuous work of controlled descent.

It was not difficult for Bob and the others to follow our route, for Roger's hands were also bleeding. Strangely the coarse surface of the ice did not feel cold that day.

Using two short ropes joined together, we descended a cliff below the tumbled section and found to our dismay evidence of fresh falls across the entire width of the glacier. Only immediately beneath the cliff was there a narrow couloir of smooth unlittered ice and here we rested briefly, flinching as each successive crack and rumble shook our perch.

Now at last we could see the lake, or rather that half of it farthest away from the glacial snout, and watch the slowly floating icebergs sailing towards the outlet torrent where they jammed its mouth, fighting for release into the fast current.

Roger twiddled the radio knobs. The battery reading was low but sufficient for the short distance involved.

Johnnie replied immediately to our call. He was with the rest of his party and a large number of Norwegians watching the ice with binoculars on a high col beside the lake.

His road party had driven from Fåberg in eight hours over the moonscape pass of Grôtli.

Peter Booth was with Johnnie and his diary describes his reflections whilst observing the descent.

> . . . There were many local guides and farmers amongst us watching the little dark figures on the ice-face. I met the four experts who had tried to climb the glacier three days before. It had taken them twenty-four hours, they had had a slight accident, and had been forced to abandon the attempt before reaching the final 1,000-foot pitch.
>
> They had descended by a rock trail – possibly the route Henrik had taken.
>
> I read a local newspaper describing their feat which Henrik translated:

'The four climbers have wanted to climb the Briksdalsbre for a long time, but only this year, they say, have they pulled enough guts together to see it through. They have been climbing much around in Norway, both mountains and glaciers.

'Among glacier experts, the Briksdalsbre is said to be the most dangerous one in Norway, and this is no doubt the reason that it has been left so much in peace by the climbers.

'The four soon discovered that the least dangerous area was the centre where there were less avalanches. The glacier was full of cracks, the biggest ninety feet deep and thirty feet wide. They had to descend deep inside some in order to pass. In places the ice was so solid that they could not use regular nails, but they were well equipped . . .'

On meeting these four climbers, I asked them what they thought of our team's chances. It was dangerous, they said, there were too many avalanches and anyway technically it was difficult even for experienced climbers. Did our party have all the right equipment? I said they had many feet of rope but no ice screws.

This was not wise, they said. If they were to make the descent, they would try to climb up it first to find the best route and then come down. But to descend it unseen; that was most unwise.

Overall, the locals gave our team little chance of getting down alive. Either the avalanches would get them or lack of the right equipment would. This was not very cheering but I was not unduly perturbed at this stage.

Watching the painful progress of the small figures down the glacier was an exciting experience.

There was the feeling that at any moment falling ice would obliterate them. They were at the glacier's mercy no matter what route they selected and by the lake the crowd of Norwegians and tourists watched in silence: the tension had communicated itself to them. Someone with binoculars had noticed a rope hanging near the top of the glacier, presumably abandoned the day before. I wondered how much rope they had left; perhaps they would not have enough equipment to complete the descent: then what?

The sun was moving on to the very face of the ice as we

watched. By using binoculars I could almost identify the individuals. It was like a cine-film. Suddenly there was a tremendous cracking noise followed by a rumble: huge lumps of ice were rolling down the glacier, shattering and jumping as they went and triggering off further falls. At the sides, avalanches rolled down with regularity. It was the speed that was terrifying to watch: within seconds of the first crack and boom, tons of ice went bouncing and sweeping down the almost vertical slopes. Anyone in the path of these falls would have stood little chance. During the morning none of our team were hit, though on occasions, I saw ice-blocks pass uncomfortably close to them, blotting them from view . . .

On our ledge the sun was making itself felt through the weight of our sweaters and anoraks. We rolled our sleeves up and drunk our fill from the dripping ice. There was a feeling of unreality about that morning.

Bob, squatting on his rucksack next to a dozing Patrick, muttered to no one in particular, 'I imagine it must be a similar feeling being under mortar fire for hours on end. You never know when or where the next one's going to land. Wherever you are, you're probably going to get crunched, so you might as well forget about your problems and relax.'

I digested this philosophy and, not being a yoga expert, decided I would relax only on reaching firm ground well out of range of the moving ice. Glancing at the others, I thought Bob showed signs, unlike the rest of us, of actually enjoying himself. Each man's make-up is different and Bob quite simply felt at home on the ice, enjoying its unpredictable quality. Once irrevocably committed he stopped thinking about the precarious nature of our position and just got on with the task.

Reading through his notes on the expedition later, I noticed that Bob had given considerable thought as to the varied motives that drove each one of us. He felt that personal background had little effect on a man's reasons for proving himself: illegitimacy might help to trigger off the ambition of a Lawrence but he did not think the vagaries of our respective parents had impelled any of us on to the ice; three of us came from military families, one had a mining father and one's was a steelworker. This he felt had influenced us little. Rather it was our individual outlooks on life that had prompted our presence on the glacier.

During a life-span there are highlights in every one's memories which they try to recapture: some get their kicks from drugs, perversions or financial gain; others from conquering the elements for the thrill of it. And the more hostile those elements, the more treasured will be the memory of dangers narrowly avoided.

Falling away beneath us for some seven hundred feet, an ice-wall of great frozen chunks reached down to the lake. Webbing the ice was a maze of wide crevasses, sometimes bridged by smaller spoil, often spanned by the balanced fragments of fractured pinnacles. These were sharply edged; the sun's rays glinting from their translucent blue to glitter like a myriad sapphires. The beauty of it all was marred only by its animation. It quivered and groaned as we watched, new crevasses opening as covering fragments slid away, others disappearing beneath unseen falls. The whole tongue grumbled ceaselessly with a continually altered cadence. Yet this was the same ice-cliff I had observed in March when it rose silent and still into the mist.

Geoff felt we would only pass this lethal region in relative safety by firm speedy action. He had a 400-foot length of thin red Marlow Terylene and, while he checked and uncoiled it, we hacked away at the base of our ledge, axing narrow grooves to anchor the rope as firmly as possible.

In the absence of ice-screws, home-made 'bollards' were a relatively safe alternative.

The rope made ready, we hurled it into the abyss. For fifty feet it was visible, snaking straight beneath us, then it disappeared over a bulging shoulder.

Henrik's voice came over the radio then, advising us that the rope had snagged in a deep crevasse: anyone descending it would be trapped. Geoff tried again, this time throwing well to the right of the ledge. Henrik confirmed that the rope now lay free, its end hidden from his view but in the area of a firm shoulder only three hundred feet above the lake.

That abseil was possibly the most perilous passage of the descent, spanning as it did some four hundred feet of broken ice, which might or might not hold firm at each descending bound of our roped bodies. We went down wearing our rucksacks, for these could not be lowered separately in safety.

Bob and I reached the hard shoulder without mishap and descended another fifty metres clear of the rope-end for safety's sake. The abseil had seemed endless and my arms and shoulders felt raw on releasing the rope. The others were invisible for a while, then Patrick appeared sliding down the rope at speed, bouncing off protruding ice pinnacles, until he approached the rope-end and I saw his hand snap across his belly halting his descent abruptly. Geoff came next, and Roger appeared over the lip as Geoff reached the central marked tag. They were sliding easily, smoothly down, when – without warning – a wide area of the ice-face between them teetered briefly, as though in slow motion, and then, as a numbing roar sounded its onslaught, came rushing down the gully towards us.

Roger disappeared, then Geoff – still swinging down the rope – was blotted from view, and briefly I glimpsed Patrick flinging himself flat as the great mass of ice rolled over his ledge, cascading down the couloir to our immediate right.

In the silence which followed, as the shock began to register, I saw Patrick's head rise from a narrow cranny. He waved at us briefly but stayed warily in his refuge.

Relief flooded my mind as I saw the thin red strand swinging wildly above us, the two sliding bodies still fixed to its length though dangling to and fro as though on a pendulum.

Geoff's language was imaginative when he reached us. The fall had been from below Roger, but it had briefly engulfed Geoff, sweeping him sideways with violence. He had lost his grip on the abseil and was held only to the rope by its friction against his anorak and by his waist carabiner. He was lucky to be alive but we were all badly unnerved. The lake was close now and the very proximity of success seemed to amplify the dangers.

A sheer bluff of ice now lay before us. It was not more than fifteen feet high but had no possible belay point above it. With great care we hacked tiny ledges for our crampons and slowly edged our way downwards.

Some way past the bluff, I was belaying Bob down a gully chimney when a scream of agony came from above. I braced myself for the explosion of ice-falls sympathetic to the sound vibrations but none came.

Leaving Bob, I retraced our route to the bluff. The other three were bunched together in a huddle at the base of the bluff.

Something was badly wrong for the snow was red with blood around them. Patrick was pressing ice against Geoff's leg and Roger unravelling a dirty bandage.

There were tears of pain in Geoff's eyes and his face was deathly pallid beneath its veneer of grime.

It transpired that Patrick had been swung off balance by his rucksack as he edged down the face of the bluff. He had fallen on to the ledge below where Geoff was waiting and one wildly flailing crampon had dug a metal spike into Geoff's skin, scraping down along the bone.

Apart from the pain, Geoff found he could still limp effectively once we lightened his load, but it was obvious he could no longer attempt any difficult obstacles or crevasses. Patrick's rucksack had broken the force of his fall which had been further softened by his belay to Roger.

We were no more than fifty yards from the last magnificent wall of blue-white ice which falls as a single sheet to the lake, but between us and its crest lay a series of broad crevasses splitting the entire width of the glacier. With Geoff limping, we would be hard pushed to negotiate any one of these fissures.

Calling for advice from below, we were counselled by Henrik to move to the left flank of the snout and descend on to the steep slipway which runs between *bergschrund* and crevasse-field.

Henrik warned us of its character,

'It is a steep shoot of loose ice and muddy slime lying over a smooth surface. All day we have watched successive avalanches channelled from above crash down it into the lake. But if you wait for a calm spell and go across fast, one by one, you will reach the ledge of rock which flanks it.'

'What happens when we get on the ledge?' asked the ever-practical Bob, 'it looks like a dead-end to me.'

But Henrik had thought that out too. 'Its far end is directly above the lake, perhaps two hundred feet above it. If you have rope left, abseil down and we will collect you by boat.'

Geoff was nodding his head affirmatively, so we set off, soon reaching the treacherous slipway. It was deeply gouged by the marks of major ice-falls and a thick alluvial mud oozed slowly downwards like lava flow as we watched.

Two ice-falls sounded high above, and we watched anxiously as the avalanche spoil hurtled by, bounding down the dark chute as though it were a skittle alley.

One by one we moved over the treacherous slope, as fast as we dared and the loose surface allowed.

Bob, who came last, was slow for his half crampon found little to grip and twice he crashed over on his side held only by his axe and our rope. As Bob joined us at the far edge of the chute, God had the last word, a sort of Amen to a day of pent-up tension. An ear-splitting roar shattered the stillness of the ravine and a pulsating rumble as of demons stirring the hot rocks of hell came out of the gathering gloom of dusk.

Then the whole grey slipway shuddered under a deluge of rushing ice-spoil as though it were a railway vibrating beneath a passing express.

'Al Hamdu lillah,' muttered Patrick, voicing the relief and gratitude we all felt. The rock was firm and reassuring beneath us as Roger hammered in a piton to secure the final rope.

TEN

Escape in the Cataracts

REACTION BEGAN TO SET in as we landed on the far side of the lake amongst a small crowd of reporters, television men, and locals, all interested to see the faces of the little orange figures they had watched for the past two days.

Rosh and Vanda proffered us flasks of soup and Mars bars and Johnnie produced a bottle of brandy. The food and liquor were very welcome, the spate of questions from reporters was not.

We left the heavy rucksacks with the rubber boat under a boulder and followed Henrik down a steep rock-strewn path running away from the lake and down the gorge. I listened to the roar of the river in the deep ravine beside us, we would certainly be travelling fast down that in our Redshanks, and as we crossed over by a little wooden bridge I glimpsed a majestic waterfall which looked too big a drop for a rubber boat to navigate.

Three miles below the lake at the upper end of the road from Olden was Johnnie's camp. The Land-Rovers and tents nestled in a grassy field close by the wooden *saeter* house of Lars Kvamme. Lars owned the red-roofed log restaurant perched above the rock canyon of the river and he gave us a great welcome when we

The gloves wore through and on the second day we were climbing with bleeding hands.

Shortly after the first descent of the notorious Briksdalsbre. *From left to right:* Roger Chapman, Bob Powell, Ranulph Fiennes, Geoff Holder, Patrick Brook.

Above the falls.

Caught in a whirlpool the rear man almost disappears as the craft's stern is sucked into the vortex.

arrived, inviting us all into his restaurant, along with the Norwegian reporters.

Lars knew more about the Briksdal area than anyone else and he now readily admitted that he had made gloomy forecasts of our doom during the two preceding days and indeed had wagered with some of Johnnie's party that we would probably never reach the upper arm of the Briksdalsbre and if we did we would be crushed during the ensuing descent.

We sat at a long banqueting table of thick undulating pine. The floor and the rafters were of pine, and the quaint bead bracelets of the two plump waitresses in their folk costumes were of alternating shades of pine carving. The low cosy room had a Hansel and Gretel air about it.

I drank five pints of fresh milk during the evening. Bob and Geoff each doubled my intake but with lager, not 'cow juice' as Bob scathingly called it.

A curling blue haze of cigar smoke filled the room, Lars found an accordion and his son struck up on a harpsichord. Henrik joined in with a mouth-organ, though the resulting noise was somewhat discordant since his lips were still cracked and blistered.

Norwegian folk songs vied with Newcastle rugby ditties and soon Bob Powell was performing a strange jig of his own with the plumper of the two waitresses. A rejuvenated Patrick, replete once more, danced an immaculate Charleston to the tune of Auld Lang Syne.

'When will you be ready to start tomorrow, d'you think?' It was John Collins of I.T.N. with his mouth full of excellent goat's cheese.

I was dozing off with heavy eyelids and could think of nothing but sleep, wondering only if I could force myself out of the warm room and down to the tents by the river.

'How d'you mean, John? Tomorrow's the day of rest with a capital R.'

A reporter from the *Bergens Tidende* – one of the national dailies – sat next to John; an attractive woman with impeccable English. She too seemed impatient.

'But will you not go down the river tomorrow morning as planned?' she asked. 'We have come a long way to record the event. You can't let us down. There are men from the national

T.V. and from the Oslo papers up here too who will be very dismayed if the river journey is put off now you have got here without incident.'

'Ruth is right, Ran, many people will be disappointed if nothing happens tomorrow.' It was Erik Berglund speaking: he worked for the *Bergens Tidende* too but was taking photographs for *The Sunday Times* since we still had no official photographer.

Filled with relief at leaving the Jostedal in safety, I had not given much thought to the daunting prospect of the river descent. After all its main purpose had originally been to transport the heavy stores from the lake to the road-head. Now that much of the equipment was lost and some twelve hundred feet of rope hung abandoned on the ice-cliff, our sole remaining task was to test the mettle of our Redshanks on the hitherto un-navigated waters of the Briksdalsbre. But I had hoped for at least two days rest after the ice descent before beginning the river phase; not realising that the photographers and John Collins would be in such a hurry.

I thought of last night on the freezing ledge, of the previous night on the open glacier and longed for sleep. Still we had promised all our sponsors the river descent as part of the programme and, since without sponsors the expedition would never have got off the ground, we owed them a great deal and must fulfil our obligations. Moreover, we had promised the Avon Rubber Company, not only that we would test their specially modified boats but that these boats would be seen being tested on all the films and documentaries resulting from the expedition. Indeed should they prove their worth, I hoped that they might let me have two to take on a 2,000-mile river journey in British Columbia which was scheduled for spring 1971.

'I must get back to London with some really good film of the river descent by tomorrow evening in time for the Ten-o'clock News,' remarked John Collins, 'and that will mean leaving by charter plane soon after midday. If you can start from the lake at, say ten o'clock, we'll all be happy.'

The others nodded their agreement and I said we would start out as soon as we could, but I wondered how the team would receive the news.

Roger was singing lustily in German and seemed quite prepared for an early start. The others were equally keen to get to grips with the river. We felt that it would be easy after the rigours of the ice-face.

Groping through the dark field I found the tents and a vacant camp-bed. Sleep came at once.

* * *

It seemed but a few minutes later when Roger shook me awake. The warm hiss of bacon sizzling outside the tent and the rush of water passing below induced me to crawl out of bed, finding my limbs unusually stiff and hands throbbing painfully though Henrik had cleaned and bound them the evening before.

Patrick was already up, warming his fingers and chewing a sausage. He wore an incongruous tweed cap and mauve corduroy jeans. Roger took one look and bade us all change into our unpleasantly damp frog-suits, reminding us to sprinkle our bodies liberally with foot-powder under the rubber to prevent chafing.

Geoff looked ghastly and limped heavily but he was determined to see the expedition through and carefully drew the black rubber suit over the bandages around his ribs and shin. Bob appeared, hearty as ever, muttering appreciative comments about the thoroughness of Norwegian hospitality. Delving into the back of a Land-Rover, he extricated new inflatable waistcoats for us all, fibre-glass crash helmets of various bright colours and four walkie-talkies of an army pattern.

We had earlier decided to ask Peter Booth to augment the climbing crew for the river descent as we would need three men to a boat and he was both experienced in the Redshanks and a strong swimmer. Johnnie Muir had hoped that one of the ice team would relinquish his crew position so that he could come instead but no one would do so. Roger would steer the first Redshank with Geoff and Patrick as crew; I would take the second with Bob and Peter paddling up front. Although the steersman acts as skipper and shouts the orders, the front men bear the brunt of the bigger waves. Even in Wales we had found that whereas the skipper might come unscathed through the curling waves below a weir, the others usually suffered a ducking on initial impact.

By nine o'clock, with a dozen Norwegians to help, the crews, looking like space-men in their helmets, set off for the lake carrying the second spare boat. I joined Roger and we cut away from the track to the ravine to get our first close look at the river itself. The growing thunder of the cascades as we approached the cliffs which imprison the cataracts made it difficult to hear Roger's comments.

I was only with him to see the various problems we would meet, to memorise the boulders, the whirlpools and the bends. The decisions as to which waterfalls were possible and which out of the question were up to Roger, the expert. Above the 200-foot waterfall we had passed the evening before, we ran into thick bush which grew to the very banks and ripped at our rubber suits as we tried to force a way through. We were perhaps a mile from the lake and had not time to find another way of reaching the river, for the others would be waiting for us and John Collins no doubt worrying about missing his aeroplane that afternoon.

Roger shouted in my ear that we would have to stop well clear of this main waterfall. He thought there were undoubtedly others but that from the lie of the land there could be no other major one between this and the lake. He decided that he would go first in Charity and stop before the waterfall. He would then throw me a safety line as we went past in case we failed to stop in time. We would have our walkie-talkie available in case of a last-minute change in plan.

Somehow the water, rough as it was, appeared to lack the lurking unpredictable power of the ice. It seemed almost an anticlimax after the last two days. Yet death came closer that morning than at any other time during the expedition. The grip of those icy waters was far more powerful than any of us had foreseen.

Half a mile from the lake, the low bushes cleared and we caught a glimpse of the river. An unexpectedly powerful volume of dark rushing water spilled in full spate over a narrow ridge, spewing geysers of spray upwards where it surged into the scattered boulders beneath. Where the water reached its new level below the cascade it formed a deep trough with a high surging wall of water thrown up beyond it.

We stopped close by and Roger threw a log which landed above the fall.

'Watch it now,' he shouted, 'you see how it's caught in the powerful current, whipped downwards into the vortex and disappears.

'There it is again trapped in the master-wave. That's what we call a hydraulic. You don't want to spend too long in one of those by yourself but if you hang on to the boat you should be all right, for the Redshanks are big and flat enough to miss the undertow.'

As I watched, the log rushed up on to the crest of the wave only to be thrown back into the trough and sucked under again. The process repeated itself whilst I watched with morbid fascination.

Then Roger was off, calling me to follow him, the long calf-knife jigging in its sheath as he ran.

The frog-suit clung tight and sweat poured from my brow as I plodded after him.

* * *

The warm rubber stench, the chafing tug at my crutch and armpits reminded me of the last time I had run pell-mell in a frog-suit, though under less reputable circumstances.

In the early sixties, a couple of years after I had left Eton, a small group of Old Etonians drove down to the adjacent town of Windsor with a carload of frog-suits, aqualungs and coils of rope. It was the night of June 3rd.

On the Fourth of June Eton celebrates its annual Founder's Day with a number of sporting events and exhibitions which in those days used to culminate with a nocturnal procession of rowing boats floodlit on the Thames. Later there were fireworks. The procession took place opposite a little island known as Luxmore's Garden. On the Eton bank a large fenced field would be filled by literally thousands of the boys' friends, relations, and girl-friends. On the Windsor bank the fields would fill with just as many Windsor citizens and tourists.

One thing which the spectators of both banks had in common, apart from wanting to watch the fireworks, was the burning desire to see one, or better still several, of the rowing boats over-balance and submerge, soaking their precocious little occupants – something which unfortunately seldom happened.

It was to satisfy the aforesaid desire that our little group furtively visited Luxmore's Garden at midnight on June 3rd. Aqualungs, flippers and rubber suits were left concealed by the low weeping willows and two of the 'frogmen' submerged with the ropes and a long pole. Floating to a point in the river opposite the central 'grandstand' seats on the Eton bank the pole was driven into the deep sludge of the river bed and a line of rope fixed from it and back to the willows of the island, well below the surface of the water.

The preparations complete, the shadowy group left the river to return – via the Windsor bank – the following evening.

No one worried when three people began to swim around shortly before dusk, since the day was still hot and close. Soon they were forgotten and, unnoticed, disappeared below the willows of the island.

With the coming of darkness, floodlights were switched on, focused on the dancing lilt of the smoothly flowing Thames.

There was a great hush amongst the assembled throng as the first boat appeared silently from behind the island. The treble tones of the little cox squeaked orders and, one by one, the gaily-clothed crew of eight stood up on their seats, lifted their long oars until they stood vertical, and wonder of wonders, doffed their straw 'boater' hats, albeit unsteadily, in the Headmaster's general direction, before sinking with relief back into their seats and rowing off. An unconvincing cheer rose from the banks.

The applause dwindled as successive boats performed their naval acrobatics and left unscathed. Then it happened. An 'eight' had arrived, its crew arisen, and the last oar had just reached the vertical, when the boat seemed to lurch. Its crew teetered – striving desperately to fend off disgrace – but too late; they were over with their garlanded straw 'boaters' bobbing like ducks. The crowds roared their approval and the shouts of 'Bravo' and 'Encore' died away only when the next boat arrived as though nothing had happened.

No one was worried for the boats could not actually sink and all the crews were strong swimmers. As soon as the stricken crew reached the edge of the floodlit area they would be picked up by waiting rowing boats.

But, to the general delight, a second boat tipped over, and, just when parents were whispering about this being the record since the 1920s, an overall uproar announced the dunking of yet another.

Careful observers then noticed a strange occurrence. Amongst the fleet of floating straw 'boaters' an alien head popped up wearing a large glass mask, and its owner began swimming with haste away from the glare of the floodlights.

A rowing boat crewed by bewildered schoolmasters saw the mask and, with shouts of anger, gave chase.

All had been going swimmingly in the friendly Thames. I had just been 'relieved' by a fellow-frogman when without warning my breathing apparatus went haywire and became unmanageable. I shot to the surface into the blinding glare of the lights and made for the nearest dark bank for a boat was approaching fast and overhauling me. Fortunately the low sweeping willows soon provided friendly obscurity, but a hue and cry had started along the bank: one was between the devil and the deep blue sea. Dropping the cumbersome oxygen bottle in some reeds, I made for the playing fields, cursing the clinging frog-suit as the thudding of many feet grew closer. Experiencing the panic of a fox run to ground I made for an aqueduct known as Fifteen Arch Bridge. A typical Eton misnomer, it has but three arches and a black oily pool alongside. With heart hammering away, I made the pool and vanished to allow the 'hounds' past. Good luck to them, I thought with momentary satisfaction; they will miss the fireworks.

Social trends and the large annual 'fireworks budget' forced the traditional ceremony to cease after that year but at least we had helped the last of the Boat Processions to be a memorable one.

* * *

I plodded on to the lake. The previous evening it had been almost clear and smooth: now its surface was littered with icebergs, some standing several feet high above the water. They were concentrated mainly at the confluence of the river, awaiting egress at its bottle-neck.

Collins and a number of photographers were discussing the merits of various camera positions; the crews worked to check the boat stowage and their own safety gear. I wondered if it was wise to allow Geoff downriver. He was limping painfully and sat apart from the others, saying little.

Roger gathered us for a final briefing on the main problems he had seen during our quick reconnaissance. He explained that over a mile of very turbulent water lay between the lake and the first major waterfall. Conditions deteriorated rapidly after leaving the lake and there was a strong chance that one or both boats might overturn. He warned us that we might find capsize drills more difficult here than in Wales because of the pounding we would receive from rocks. He was about to say more, when he checked himself and with a brief mutter about keeping the cameramen waiting he left us, accompanied by his crew.

Roger's diary shows that all went well to begin with:

. . . there is something very exciting in pushing off down a steep river knowing full well that once you have committed yourself, there can be no turning back. This sort of white-water riding is somewhat similar to riding a bobsleigh on the Cresta Run, except you are not quite so much in control of your mount.

The feeling is something between surf-riding and shooting down a helter-skelter at a fairground, except of course, one is going head first. Once through the region of icebergs, we dropped over a water chute, spun to the left and flinched as a great wave of water completely covered the craft. Our bows came crazily through the waves to drop again over another rock and into a morass of churning water. Then things began to speed up, the power of the river to assert itself . . .

Our turn came. The boat was called Faith. I found myself feeling rather nervous, apprehensive, as we pushed off from the lakeside but soon we were amongst the mêlée of grinding icebergs with no time for anything but the awkward navigation of tons of mobile ice.

Once through, the current caught us, spinning the boat around in an eddy so that we were back to front for the first mad descent of a frothing chute. As we dropped, water churned over the side walls but this was forgotten as we hit the hydraulic wave below.

Since we were backwards the water hit me first lifting me bodily from the steering compartment and sweeping me violently on to my stomach between the others. Both were crouching flat, gripping the hand-slings. The water surged over us and we came through into a confusing area of many racing chutes, split by giant boulders.

'We'll take the main chute slightly left,' I shouted.

It was in fact quite out of the question to steer for any of the other routes, but there seemed no harm in bolstering the crew's confidence in their skipper.

The alarming truth was that the current ran far stronger than during our Welsh practice sessions and my frantic attempts at steering were having very little response from the bucking Faith, full of water as she was.

As always in fast-moving water there is little time to react. Thus, when a submerged rock caught the craft amidships, and held us across the main bore, Faith flipped over and we came up alongside gasping for breath, forgetting all we had ever learnt about capsize drills. I felt a sharp pain in the knee as it battered against a rock.

Faith was moving fast now, upside down but facing the right way and buoyant without the weight of captive water. I thought briefly of the radio and other kit, but it was stowed carefully in the waterproof zipper-thwarts and should be safe enough.

Bob and Peter were back with the upside down boat, lying up front and gripping the canvas straps.

I tried shouting to them, but could hardly hear my own voice. We were moving very rapidly now, totally in the grip of the main deluge.

It must be unpleasant at the front, I remember thinking, for with Faith upside down we could do nothing but cling on and brace ourselves as each successive cataract received us, sending a series of waves over Faith which enveloped us utterly with little interim respite.

I felt a nudging fear as I saw a blur of colour on the bank to the right. There were tourists all along the rocks now. They passed merely as blurred images in our wild passage through a nightmarish series of corkscrew hydraulics. We gulped air into our starved lungs and cowered as each new wave curled ahead and smashed over us. Sometimes we moved sideways, sometimes backwards, but the little craft kept going.

We must have come a good mile, I thought, where the hell is Charity? Roger definitely said he would stop well short of the waterfalls and they can't be too far away now. How the devil are we going to stop in this lot? I glanced at the banks to try and remember some landmark but my head was forced down on to the neoprene hull as a wave covered us.

We had become an amorphous part of the maelstrom, our ears accustomed to the overall roar of the falling waters but now a new sound was introduced, or rather there came a change in the volume of the existing tumult. From somewhere ahead came the sound of thunder, a fluctuating boom which could only mean one thing.

From the corner of my eye I spotted Charity high and dry on a cluster of rocks in mid-river. Roger was there with a coil of rope. As we passed he flung it high above us, the white line snaking out over Faith.

Bob had seized the thick cord with one hand and I watched as he desperately tied a reef-knot to secure it to the boat-strap between Peter and himself before the line snapped taut with the weight of the craft.

For a moment I thought he had succeeded, for the boat shuddered of a sudden and whipped round about to career amid the raging waters at the end of the taut line.

By rights Faith should have swung on the rope-end with the action of a pendulum so that we might reach the bank. But for some reason she caught stubbornly amid the wild vortex and I knew something would soon break with the strain.

Bob's feet were threshing in front of me. I glanced up to find his face contorted with pain and Peter's free hand scrabbling at the reef-knot where rope joined canvas strap. Bob's hand, or maybe only a couple of his fingers, had caught in the rope somehow and now the whole weight of the bucking craft caused the nylon to cut into Bob's skin, crushing the nerves.

Grasping the long knife from my leg-sheath, I crawled over Peter's legs and back to cut the rope free. After all, it was only causing a temporary stay of execution: whatever happened now we should have to jump clear and try to reach either bank before the waterfall claimed us. Just before the rope was severed, it went suddenly slack and Faith was away.

I screamed 'Jump for it, jump clear' at the top of my lungs, and watched Peter and Bob, the latter now clear of the rope, dive towards the rocks by the right-hand bank.

As I crouched before springing off, the boat spun sideways round a sharp curve and, buoyant with its lighter load, was violently ejected on to the low rocks at the crown of the bend.

I lay dazed for a moment in an ungainly sprawl atop the sturdy Faith.

'We thought you were off for a lone free-fall over the waterfall.'

It was Peter and Bob who came slithering along the bank. They too had been ejected on the corner and were bruised but otherwise unhurt by their immersion. One of Bob's fingers had been badly crushed at the joint and he now held it up before him as he walked, as though making a rude sign.

Peter unearthed a rope stowed in Faith and with it we pulled the boat clear of the water. We staggered up the rocky bank there to see a large crowd gathering, as crowds do when disaster appears imminent.

Henrik had just finished attending to Geoff who by all accounts had nearly drowned, saved only by quick action on the part of Roger and an English tourist, a Harrow School geography master called Tony Escritt who gave me his version of the near-fatal incident.

Tony had watched Charity manage to land on a little island of rocks and fling a line to Faith. He could not see the trouble with Bob's finger but he watched as Charity's crew struggled to hold the line which was belayed around Geoff and held firm by Roger and Patrick.

The strain had been too great and Roger was dragged slowly forwards. He had shouted back to warn Geoff that they must let go. Geoff tried to do so but the rope snagged round his neck and shoulder as the front two let go and jerked him bodily into the waves.

The remainder of the flailing line dragged Roger and Patrick in too, though Patrick managed to clasp a small rock in mid-stream, held there by the rope curled around his leg.

Tony Escritt watched as Geoff disappeared for a long time and, when he finally reappeared for a brief moment in mid-river, he was clearly in great difficulty and drowning. The power of the current gave the rope a pendulum motion and Geoff next appeared quite close to the bank. Tony and Roger – the latter still gasping from his own immersion – managed to grasp Geoff's head and cut the rope which held his neck. They then dragged him clear and brought him back to consciousness.

More rope was then found and Patrick, his dry humour decidedly dampened, was brought back to the bank on a line, after the manner of a salmon being played – though not as reluctant.

We decided that further navigation above the waterfall would be dangerous and returned to the Briksdal camp to lick our wounds. Johnnie volunteered to take Geoff's place in Charity for the remaining stretch of river since Geoff had to return to England the next day. Before leaving us, Geoff agreed that the expedition had been a stimulating series of 'once only' experiences and said he could hardly wait for the next 'journey', which considering all the bashes he had taken was valiant of him.

Roger in his diary, notes that '. . . It interested me to see how the members of the expedition who were involved in the first day's boat journey would find the experience of returning to the dangerous river. There was no doubt, the next day, as we made our way across the rocks and looked down into the foaming water, that there was a feeling of tension not previously experienced. Bob made no bones about it by admitting that he was scared stiff.'

But below the 200-foot sheet of falling water with its billowing pelmet of rainbow spray, the river became less severe in its rush to the fjords.

We embarked below the fall and for four miles followed the racing torrent through the lower reaches of the gorge. At first a narrow canyon gave us trouble, the waters dashing against the imprisoning walls in frenzied motion which twirled our boats and had the crews ducking low as overhanging rock threatened to batter their passing skulls. Then the canyon was behind us and the waters became more predictable.

Now Faith was responding to the steering paddle, and an enjoyable feeling of mastery over the craft came as we plunged through minor rapids steering easily through boulders and cavorting eddies. The pleasure of speed untainted by fear had us singing in discordant unison and racing the other craft past fields where hay hung on fences to dry. The slopes leaning to the warm south sported strawberry beds and fruit trees; ponies champed lucerne; ageing farmers sat warming bandy legs in the sun beneath the eaves of their compact little houses.

We passed through the tiny hamlet of Mickelbust. Boys on bicycles had been our permanent companions at the Briksdal camp and they must have spread the news of our coming, for each little bridge we passed beneath was lined with families waving to us. The kilometres sped by in this warm land of wind-blown grass and smiling faces as we bobbed our way south.

Imperceptibly the river moved more slowly now between wider banks until at last we came to a bend where the river ended and Oldenfjord stretched out before us, a smooth shining highway to the North Sea.

In a few days we would be back in England, back to the daily grind of nine till five. Occasionally reminiscing, we would savour with a delicious surge of residual tension, the memory of falling ice, the roar of pounding water or the rush of freezing air as the body plummets from ten thousand feet. Personal memories which we would hug to ourselves, knowing that they alone had made the expedition worth while, though others, the outsiders, would never understand.

But much of value had been learnt. How fast was the glacier melting or accumulating? At what speed was the Fåberg ice-tongue advancing or shrinking? What of the unseen insect life on the ice? These questions and many others would be answered when our survey and scientific research had been evaluated and our specimens and data analysed in the British Museum and the Hermitage School of Survey. Future expeditions might save time and effort using parachutes and learning from our experience. A mass of equipment had been tested under tough conditions, defects and values revealed. The Briksdal glacier had been conquered for the first time and rubber boats had shown their ability to navigate rocky defiles where current craft like canoes or kayaks would stand little chance.

Now I was content to float awhile in silence: to move quietly with the breeze on the lake whose waters mirrored the cold white peaks of the Jostedal. A world set apart from the mad bustle of the ever-spreading concrete jungle where man too easily forgets the raw power of nature and his own transient stature.

Acknowledgments

The Expedition was made possible only through the generous help of a number of persons and organisations. Without their support the venture would not have taken place and we are extremely grateful to our sponsors in Britain and Norway.

We wish to thank:

In Norway and representing Norway in Great Britain:

Mr. Erik Berglund, photographer (*Bergen Tidende*)
Mr. Brandenburger, British Leyland P.R. representative, Oslo
Mr. Jan Greve, photographer, Oslo
Mr. Eivind Grov, Manager, Hotel Alexandra, Loen
Mr. Hysing-Dahl, Manager, Westwing Air Service, Bergen
Mr. Bill Knott, Director, Bergen Line, London
Mr. Lars Kvamme, Manager, Briksdal Centre
Mr. Martin Lilleheim, journalist and friend
Mr. Inge Lodoen, Manager, Stryn Turistnemnd
Mr. Jan Mickelbust, Head guide, Briksdal area
Mr. David Mindresunde, Head guide, Loen District
Mr. Odd-Arnu, British Leyland P.R. representative, Bergen
Dr. Gunnar Østrem, Director, Hydrological Dept., Norges Vassdrags og-Elektrisitetsvesen, Oslo
Mr. Paul Paulsen, Chief pilot, Westwing Air Service, Bergen
Mr. Knut Sjovorr, Director, Norwegian Tourist Office, London
Mr. John Woods, Services Manager, Bergen Line, London

In Great Britain:

The Army School of Survey, Hermitage
Wing Commander Bowen, British Defence Attaché, Oslo
The British Museum (Natural History Dept.)
Major John Blashford-Snell of the Scientific Exploration Society
Mr. Robin Denniston, Director, Hodder and Stoughton Ltd.

Miss Susan Duncan, The River Dee Catering
Mr. E. A. Escritt, B.A.
Richard Fiennes, M.A., M.R.C.V.S.
L. G. Goodwin, M.B., B.S., M.R.C.P.
Mr. D. Keir of Whitbread & Co. Ltd.
Mr. Bob King of Little and Kings, Film Distributors
Mr. Edgar Lewy of Philart Productions Ltd., 11 Bermondsey Street, London S.E.1
Mr. Jim McEwen, Publicity Manager, Hodder and Stoughton Ltd.
Major John Peacock, F.R.G.S.
Major Brian Roberts and Captain G. C. Hopkins of H.Q. Denbigh and Flint A.C.F.
Captain Peter Rowe, The Royal Hussars
The School of Geodosy, Oxford
The Scott Polar Institute
Captain Guy Sheridan and Captain Doug Keenan, The Royal Marines
Mr. R. Shortland, British Embassy, Oslo
The Staff of Netheravon Army Parachute Centre
Sir John Walker, retired British Ambassador in Oslo
Lieutenant Colonel M. Wilcox at the Ministry of Defence
Mr. Egil Woxholt
Miss Barrie McGill of Aladdin Industries Ltd.
Mr. Ken Catt of The Avon Rubber Co. Ltd.
Mr. W. R. R. Price of Batchelors Foods Ltd.
Mr. J. S. Short of Bencard
Mr. W. B. Wilkinson of the Bovril Group Marketing Ltd.
Mr. R. H. Cornford of Brooke Bond Oxo Ltd.
Squadron Leader J. A. Cook of Burndept Electronics (E.R.) Ltd.
Mr. P. J. Crombie of G. Costa & Co. Ltd.
Miss P. F. McClintock of Glaxo
Mr. N. P. Cutcliffe of H. J. Heinz Co. Ltd.
Mr. Ben Howkins of I.D.V.
Mrs. Meacock of Lillywhites Ltd.
Mr. Eddie Hawkins of Marlow Ropes Ltd.
Mr. G. Harris of Mars Chocolate Ltd.
Mr. I. A. Howie of the Merrydown Wine Co. Ltd.
Mr. R. Hampton of the Metal Box Co. Ltd.
Mr. J. A. Ridgewell of Mitchell Cotts Services Ltd.

J. Shirley Rainer of The Nestlé Co. Ltd.
Mr. Chris Hawksworth of Northern Wild Water Centre
Mr. B. C. Snelling of Racal Electronics Ltd.
Mr. S. Hughes of The Rover Co. Ltd.
Mr. Keith Kent of The Rover Co. Ltd.
Mr. Brian Llewellyn of The Rover Co. Ltd.
Mr. Brian Sperring of The Rover Co. Ltd.
Miss Patricia Lotery of Saward, Baker & Co. Ltd.
Miss Laura Rowe of Standard Brands Ltd.
Mr. J. H. Price of Tate & Lyle & Assoc. Companies
Miss A. Stanton of Unigate Ltd.
Mr. E. J. Boote of Unilever Export Ltd.
Mr. B. J. Ward of B. J. Ward Ltd.
Mr. D. Keir of Whitbreads & Co. Ltd.
Mr. B. C. N. Snelling of Wild Heerbrugg (UK) Ltd.
Mr. P. A. Savage of The Wrigley Co. Ltd.
Yardley & Co. Ltd.

There are others who helped the expedition who are not named above, but to whom our thanks are also due. In particular, Mrs. Booth at Durrington Wells for her kindness and hospitality, to the Road Party – Vanda, Rosemary, Jane and Gillie whose cheerfulness and industry kept the wheels going round, and to Andrew Moncrieff for his long-suffering forbearance at 23G.

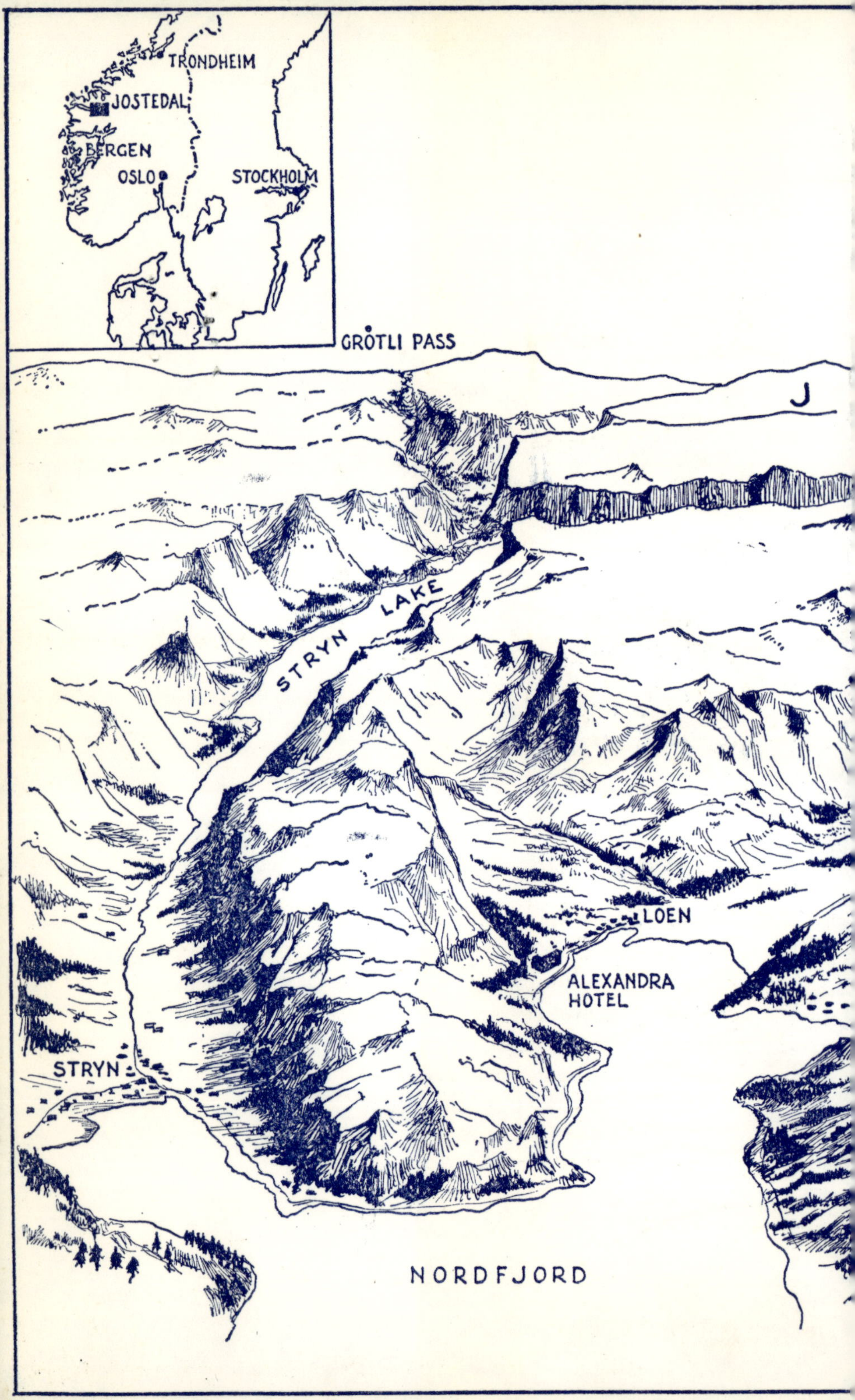
TRONDHEIM
JOSTEDAL
BERGEN
OSLO
STOCKHOLM
GRÖTLI PASS
J
STRYN LAKE
LOEN
ALEXANDRA HOTEL
STRYN
NORDFJORD